Informing the legislative debate since 1914 _____

Energy and Water Development: FY2014 Appropriations

Carl E. Behrens, Coordinator
Specialist in Energy Policy

November 1, 2013

Congressional Research Service

7-5700

www.crs.gov

R43121

Summary

The Energy and Water Development appropriations bill provides funding for civil works projects of the Army Corps of Engineers (Corps), for the Department of the Interior's Bureau of Reclamation (Reclamation), the Department of Energy (DOE), and several independent agencies.

FY2013 Energy and Water Development appropriations were considered in the context of the Budget Control Act of 2011 (BCA, P.L. 112-25), which established discretionary spending limits for FY2012-FY2021. On March 26, 2013, the President signed H.R. 933, the FY2013 Defense and Military Construction/VA, Full Year Continuing Resolution (P.L. 113-6). The act funds Energy and Water Development accounts at the FY2012 enacted level for the rest of FY2013, with some exceptions. However, under BCA, an automatic spending reduction process, consisting of a combination of sequestration and lower discretionary spending caps, went into effect March 1, 2013. The effect of these reductions on the budgetary resources that will ultimately be available to an agency at the account level remains unclear until further guidance is provided by the Office of Management and Budget as to how these reductions should be applied.

President Obama's FY2014 budget request for Energy and Water Development was released in April 2013. The request totaled $34.4 billion. On June 26 the House Appropriations Committee reported a bill, H.R. 2609, with a total of $30.4 billion; the bill passed the House, with amendments, on July 10. The Senate Appropriations Committee reported out a bill, S. 1245, on June 27, with a total of $34.4 billion. On October 16, 2013, Congress passed the Continuing Appropriations Act, 2014, H.R. 2775, P.L. 113-46, extending funding for all federal programs, including Energy and Water Development, through January 15, 2014, at the FY2013 post-sequestration spending level.

For FY2014, as in previous years, the level of overall spending will be a major issue. On March 21, 2013, the House passed H.Con.Res. 25, setting FY2014 spending at $2.77 trillion. On March 23, the Senate passed S.Con.Res. 8, with a spending level for FY2014 of $2.96 trillion. On June 4 the House Appropriations Committee issued budget allocations for the individual subcommittees (H.Rept. 113-96). The suballocation for Energy and Water Development programs was set at $30.4 billion. On June 20 the Senate Appropriations Committee announced subcommittee allocations for FY2014; the Energy and Water Development suballocation was $34.8 billion.

In addition to funding levels, issues specific to Energy and Water Development programs include

- the distribution of appropriations for Corps (Title I) and Reclamation (Title II) projects that have historically received congressional appropriations above Administration requests;

- alternatives to the proposed national nuclear waste repository at Yucca Mountain, Nevada, which the Administration has abandoned (Title III: Nuclear Waste Disposal);

- proposed FY2014 spending levels for Energy Efficiency and Renewable Energy (EERE) programs (Title III) that are more than 50% higher in the Administration's request than the amount appropriated for FY2012; and,

- funding for the nuclear weapons program and other defense activities, which make up half of the total Department of Energy budget.

Contents

Tables

Contacts

Most Recent Developments

President Obama's FY2014 budget request for Energy and Water Development was released in April 2013. The request totaled $34.4 billion. On June 18, 2013, the House Energy and Water Development Subcommittee approved a FY2014 bill totaling $30.4 billion. The bill, H.R. 2609, passed the House with amendments on July 10. The Senate Energy and Water Development Subcommittee reported out a bill June 25, totaling $34.4 billion, and the full Appropriations Committee approved the bill, S. 1245, on June 27. On October 16, 2013, Congress passed the Continuing Appropriations Act, 2014, H.R. 2775, P.L. 113-46, extending funding for all federal programs, including Energy and Water Development, through January 15, 2014, at the FY2013 post-sequestration spending level.

Status

Table 1 indicates the status of the FY2014 funding legislation. Cells will be filled in as the appropriations cycle progresses.

Table I. Status of Energy and Water Development Appropriations, FY2014

Subcommittee Markup		House Report	House Passage	Senate Report	Senate Passage	Conf. Report	Final Approval		Public Law
House	Senate						House	Senate	
6/18/13	6/25/13	H.Rept. 113-135	7/10/13	S.Rept. 113-47					

Overview

The Energy and Water Development bill includes funding for civil works projects of the U.S. Army Corps of Engineers (Corps), the Department of the Interior's Central Utah Project (CUP) and Bureau of Reclamation (Reclamation), the Department of Energy (DOE), and a number of independent agencies, including the Nuclear Regulatory Commission (NRC) and the Appalachian Regional Commission (ARC).

The Budget Control Act and Energy and Water Development Appropriations for FY2013 and FY2014

FY2013 discretionary appropriations were considered in the context of the Budget Control Act of 2011 (BCA, P.L. 112-25), which established discretionary spending limits for FY2012-FY2021. The BCA also tasked a Joint Select Committee on Deficit Reduction to develop a federal deficit reduction plan for Congress and the President to enact by January 15, 2012. Because deficit reduction legislation was not enacted by that date, an automatic spending reduction process established by the BCA was triggered; this process consists of a combination of sequestration and lower discretionary spending caps, initially scheduled to begin on January 2, 2013. The "joint committee" sequestration process for FY2013 required the Office of Management and Budget (OMB) to implement across-the-board spending cuts at the account and program level to achieve equal budget reductions from both defense and nondefense funding at a percentage to be determined, under terms specified in the Balanced Budget and Emergency Deficit Control Act of 1985 (BBEDCA, Title II of P.L. 99-177, 2 U.S.C. 900-922), as amended by the BCA. For further information on the Budget Control Act, see CRS Report R41965, *The Budget Control Act of 2011*, by Bill Heniff Jr., Elizabeth Rybicki, and Shannon M. Mahan.

The American Taxpayer Relief Act (ATRA, P.L. 112-240), enacted on January 2, 2013, made a number of significant changes to the procedures in the BCA that will take place during FY2013. First, the date for the joint committee sequester to be implemented was delayed for two months, until March 1, 2013. Second, the dollar amount of the joint committee sequester was reduced by $24 billion. Third, the statutory caps on discretionary spending for FY2013 (and FY2014) were lowered. For further information on the changes to BCA procedures made by ATRA, see CRS Report R42949, *The American Taxpayer Relief Act of 2012: Modifications to the Budget Enforcement Procedures in the Budget Control Act*, by Bill Heniff Jr.

Pursuant to the BCA, as amended by ATRA, President Obama ordered that the joint committee sequester be implemented on March 1, 2013.[1] The accompanying OMB report indicated a dollar amount of budget authority to be canceled to each account containing non-exempt funds.[2] The sequester will ultimately be applied at the program, project, and activity (PPA) level within each account.[3] Because the sequester was implemented at the time that a temporary continuing resolution was in force, the reductions were calculated on an annualized basis and will be apportioned throughout the remainder of the fiscal year.[4] Although full year FY2013 funding has been enacted, the effect of these reductions on the budgetary resources that will ultimately be available to an agency at either the account or PPA level remains unclear until further guidance is provided by OMB as to how these reductions should be applied.

The uncertainty about precise levels of sequestration during FY2013 is reflected in the reports issued by both the House and Senate Appropriations Committees for FY2014. Both reports list PPA FY2013 appropriated levels that do not reflect the sequester of March 1, 2013. In addition, the House report levels do not reflect the additional across-the-board rescission made by OMB to comply with the statutory limits as provided by Section 3004 of the FY2013 Defense and Military Construction/VA, Full Year Continuing Resolution, P.L. 113-6. In this CRS report, unless otherwise noted, figures for FY2013 appropriated amounts are those given in the Senate report, S.Rept. 113-47.

Table 2 includes budget totals for energy and water development appropriations enacted for FY2006 to FY2013.

---

[1] White House, President Obama, Sequestration Order for Fiscal Year 2013 Pursuant to Section 251A of the Balanced Budget and Emergency Deficit Control Act, As Amended, March 1, 2013, available at http://www.whitehouse.gov/sites/default/files/2013sequestration-order-rel.pdf.

[2] Executive Office of the President, Office of Management and Budget, *OMB Report to the Congress on the Joint Committee Sequestration for Fiscal Year 2013*, March 1, 2013, available at http://www.whitehouse.gov/sites/default/files/omb/assets/legislative_reports/fy13ombjcsequestrationreport.pdf.

[3] Ibid., pp. 11, 13.

[4] Ibid., p. 5. For general information on continuing resolutions, see CRS Report R42647, *Continuing Resolutions: Overview of Components and Recent Practices*, by Jessica Tollestrup.

Table 2. Energy and Water Development Appropriations, FY2007 to FY2014

(budget authority in billions of current dollars)

FY2007	FY2008	FY2009	FY2010	FY2011	FY2012	FY2013	FY2014[a]
29.4	30.9	40.5[b]	33.4	31.7	34.4[c]	32.7[d]	34.9

Source: Compiled by CRS.

Note: Figures represent current dollars, exclude permanent budget authorities, and reflect rescissions.

a. Requested budget authority.

b. Includes $7.5 billion for Advanced Technology Vehicle Manufacturing Loan Program.

c. Includes $1.7 billion in emergency funding for the Corps of Engineers.

d. Total does not include sequestration requirements of the Budget Control Act which went into effect March 1, 2013.

Table 3 lists totals for each of the bill's four titles.

Table 3. Energy and Water Development Appropriations Summary

($ millions)

Title	FY2012 Approp.	FY2013 Approp.[a]	FY2014 Request	House	Senate	Conf.
Title I: Corps of Engineers	6,726.0[b]	10,322.0[c]	4,726.0	4,898.0	5,272.0	
Title II: CUP & Reclamation	1,076.4	1,066.7	1,049.6	990.0	1,099.6	
Title III: Department of Energy	25,748.0	27,046.4	28,927.9	24,866.9	28,209.9	
Title IV: Independent Agencies	254.5	252.2	243.8	249.3	253.8	
Scorekeeping Adjustments[d]	—	-565.5	-565.5	-565.5	-565.5	
E&W Total	**35,529.0[b]**	**38,121.8[c]**	**34,381.8**	**30,438.7**	**34,269.8**	

Source: FY2014 budget request, H.Rept. 113-135, S.Rept. 113-47.

a. Source: S.Rept. 113-47. Figures do not reflect the March 1, 2013, sequester of funds under P.L. 112-25.

b. Includes $1.724 billion in supplemental funding for the Corps of Engineers under the FY2012 Disaster Relief Appropriations Act (P.L. 112-77).

c. Includes $5,350 billion in supplemental funding for the Corps of Engineers under the Disaster Relief Appropriations Act, 2013 (P.L. 113-2).

d. Includes offsetting revenues from various sources.

Tables 4 through **15** provide budget details for Title I (Corps of Engineers), Title II (Department of the Interior), Title III (Department of Energy), and Title IV (independent agencies) for FY2012-FY2013, and proposed funding for FY2014. The FY2013 figures do not reflect the March 1, 2013, sequester of funds under P.L. 112-25. Accompanying these tables is a discussion of the key issues involved in the major programs in the four titles.

Title I: Army Corps of Engineers[5]

The Energy and Water Development bill provides funding for the civil program of the U.S. Army Corps of Engineers (Corps), an agency in the Department of Defense with both military and civilian responsibilities. Under its civil works program, the Corps plans, builds, operates, and maintains a wide range of water resources facilities. The Corps attracts congressional attention because its projects can have significant local and regional economic benefits and environmental effects, in addition to their water resource development purposes.

A number of recent changes have affected Corps appropriations, including earmark moratoriums in both houses in the 112th and 113th Congress and reductions for some projects and classes of projects compared to previous years. Additionally, in recent years flooding events on the Mississippi and Missouri rivers and in the northeastern United States affected a number of Corps projects which received supplemental funds. In addition to the regular Corps appropriation for FY2012, Congress appropriated $1.724 billion in supplemental funding for response and recovery related to 2012 flooding and $5.35 billion in supplemental funding related to Hurricane Sandy.[6] (See **Table 4**.)

In most years, the President's budget request for the Corps is below the agency's enacted appropriation.[7] The final full year Continuing Resolution for FY2013 extended FY2012 enacted funding levels for the Corps, or about $4.98 billion before the sequester. The Corps subsequently released its FY2013 Work Plan, which provided final project and account level totals after the sequester.[8] According to these documents, the final post-sequester appropriation for the Corps in FY2013 was $4.718 billion.

The President's FY2014 budget request for the Corps was $4.826 billion, not accounting for proposed rescission of prior year funds. In its markup, the House Appropriations Committee recommended $4.876 billion for the Corps, or about $50 million more than the amount requested by the Administration for FY2014. The Senate Appropriations Committee recommended $5.272 billion for the Corps, or $546 million more than the Administration's request.

Earmarks and the Corps of Engineers

Corps funding is part of the debate over congressionally directed spending, or "earmarks." Unlike highways and municipal water infrastructure programs, federal funds for the Corps are not distributed to states or projects based on a formula or delivered via competitive grants. Generally about 85% of the appropriations for Corps civil works activities are directed to specific projects. In addition to specific projects identified for funding in the President's budget, in past years many Corps projects have received additional funding from Congress in the appropriations process.[9]

---

[5] This section was prepared by Charles V. Stern.

[6] Some of these funds were restricted to areas that were impacted by these storms.

[7] For instance, the FY2012 enacted appropriation for the Corps was $5.002 billion, or approximately $500 million more than the President's FY2012 request.

[8] FY2013 Work Plan documents are available at http://www.usace.army.mil/Missions/CivilWorks/Budget.aspx.

[9] While congressional earmarks make up a relatively small percentage of most agency budgets, a significant number of Corps projects have historically received additional funding from Congress for construction or operational expenditures.

Since the 112th Congress, site-specific project line items added by Congress (i.e., earmarks) have been among those projects subject to House and Senate earmark moratoriums. As a result, additional congressional funding at the project level has not been provided since FY2010. In lieu of the traditional project-based increases, Congress has included additional funding for selected categories of Corps projects (e.g., "ongoing navigation work") that were not funded in the President's budget, and provided limited direction to the Corps for allocation of these funds.[10] The House and Senate both continued this practice in their FY2014 recommendations.

Table 4. Energy and Water Development Appropriations
Title I: Army Corps of Engineers

($ millions)

Program	FY2012 Approp.	FY2012 Supp[a]	FY2013 Supp[b]	FY2013 Enacted[c]	FY2014 Request	House	Senate	Conf.
Investigations and Planning	117.0	-	50.0	124.8	90.0	90.0	120.0	
Construction	1,617.0	-	3,461.0	1,670.7	1,350.0	1,343.0	1,542.0	
Mississippi River & Tributaries (MR&T)	252.0	802.0	-	251.5	200.0	249.0	300.0	
Operation and Maintenance (O&M)	2,412.0	534.0	821.0	2,407.2	2,588.0	2,682.0	2,700.0	
Regulatory	193.0	-	-	192.6	279.0	193.0	200.0	
General Expenses	185.0	-	-	184.6	182.0	182.0	182.0	
FUSRAP[d]	109.0	-	-	108.8	104.0	104.0	195.0	

---

[10] Congress provided additional funding and guidance for several broad categories of projects in the FY2012 conference report (H.Rept. 112-331), and these allocations were carried over by reference in FY2013's long term continuing resolution. The FY2012 report instructed the Corps to make project level allocations in a "work plan" and report back to Congress. Some of the categories to be funded in the work plan were designated by Congress as only being available for projects which were not included in the Administration's budget request. Recent Work Plan allocations are available at http://www.usace.army mil/Missions/CivilWorks/Budget.aspx.

Program	FY2012 Approp.	FY2012 Supp[a]	FY2013 Supp[b]	FY2013 Enacted[c]	FY2014 Request	House	Senate	Conf.
Flood Control & Coastal Emergencies (FC&CE)	112.0	388.0	1,008.0	26.9	28.0	28.0	28.0	
Office of the Asst. Secretary of the Army	5.0	-	10.0	5.0	5.0	5.0	5.0	
Total Title I	**5,002.0**	**1,724.0**	**5,350.0**	**4,972.0**	**4,726.0**[e]	**4,876.0**	**5,272.0**	

Source: FY2014 budget request, H.Rept. 113-135, S.Rept. 113-47.

Notes:

a. $1.724 billion in supplemental funding was provided under the FY2012 Disaster Relief Appropriations Act (P.L. 112-77) for flooding in the Midwestern United States, among other things.

b. $5.35 billion in supplemental funding related to the consequences of Hurricane Sandy was provided under the Disaster Relief Appropriations Act, 2013 (P.L. 113-2).

c. Source: S.Rept. 113-47. Figures do not reflect the March 1, 2013, sequester of funds under P.L. 112-25.

d. Formerly Utilized Sites Remedial Action Program.

e. The Administration's request included a $100 million rescission from formerly appropriated funds, which was not included by the House or Senate.

Key Policy Issues—Corps of Engineers

Project Backlog and New Starts

The large number of authorized Corps projects that have not received appropriations to date, or that are authorized and have received funding but are incomplete, is often referred to as the "backlog" of authorized projects. Estimates of the backlog range from $11 billion to more than $80 billion, depending on which projects are included (e.g., those that meet Administration budget criteria, those that have received funding in recent appropriations, those that have never received appropriations). The backlog raises policy questions, such as whether there is a disconnect between the authorization and appropriations processes, and how to prioritize among authorized activities.[11]

Recent budget requests by the Administration have included few new studies and construction starts, and enacted appropriations for FY2011, FY2012, and FY2013 barred any funding for new projects (defined as projects or studies that have not received appropriations previously). For FY2014, the Administration requested funding for four new construction starts and 10 new studies.[12] The House Appropriations Committee recommended no funding for New Starts in

---

[11] For more information, see CRS Report R41243, *Army Corps of Engineers: Water Resource Authorizations, Appropriations, and Activities*, by Nicole T. Carter and Charles V. Stern

[12] The FY2014 proposed new starts are Hamilton City, CA (Ecosystem Restoration); Lower Colorado River Basin, TX (Flood Risk Management); Louisiana Coastal Area, LA (Ecosystem Restoration); Columbia River, OR and WA (continued...)

FY2014. The Senate Appropriations Committee agreed with the Administration's request and recommended that the Corps produce a list of an additional five new studies and three new construction starts in its Work Plan for FY2014.

Navigation Trust Funds

In addition to regular appropriations, two congressionally authorized "trust funds" are administered by the Corps and require annual appropriations. The Harbor Maintenance Trust Fund and the Inland Waterway Trust Fund support cost shared investments in federal navigation infrastructure and have both received attention in recent years. While the Harbor Maintenance Trust Fund has a surplus balance, the Inland Waterway Trust Fund currently faces a shortfall and a curtailment of activities. Both trust funds are discussed below.

Harbor Maintenance Trust Fund

In 1986, Congress enacted the Harbor Maintenance Tax (HMT) to recover operation and maintenance (O&M) costs at U.S. coastal and Great Lakes harbors from maritime shippers. O&M is mostly the dredging of harbor channels to their authorized depths and widths. The tax is levied on importers and domestic shippers using coastal or Great Lakes ports. The tax revenues are deposited into the Harbor Maintenance Trust Fund (HMTF) from which Congress appropriates funds for harbor dredging.

In 1990, Congress increased the HMT rate from 4 cents per $100 of cargo value to 12.5 cents per $100 of cargo value in the Omnibus Budget Reconciliation Act (P.L. 101-508). In recent years, HMTF annual expenditures have remained relatively flat while HMT collections have increased due to rising import volume.[13] Consequently, a large surplus in the HMTF has developed. The maritime industry seeks to enact a "spending guarantee" to spend down the surplus in the HMTF (see H.R. 335 and S. 218). Some harbor channels are reportedly not being maintained at their authorized depth and width, requiring ships with the deepest drafts to "light load" or wait for high tide. Harbors primarily used by fishing vessels or recreational craft have also complained of insufficient maintenance dredging. Since spending from the HMTF requires an appropriation from Congress, spending more from the HMTF could reduce available funding for other Energy and Water Development activities under congressional budget caps.

The Administration's FY2014 budget requested $890 million from the HMTF, leaving an estimated-end-of-year balance of more than $8.9 billion. The House Appropriations Committee recommended $1 billion for HMTF expenditures, or $110 million more than the Administration's request. The Senate Appropriations Committee did not specify an overall funding level for the HMTF in its markup.

For more information on harbor maintenance funding, see CRS Report R41042, *Harbor Maintenance Trust Fund Expenditures*, by John Frittelli.

(...continued)

(Navigation).

[13] The exception was 2009, when collections declined along with import volume.

Inland Waterway Trust Fund

Since the 1980s, expenditures for construction and major rehabilitation projects on inland waterways have been cost-shared on a 50/50 basis between the federal government and users through the Inland Waterway Trust Fund (IWTF).[14] IWTF monies derive from a fuel tax on commercial vessels on designated waterways, plus investment interest on the balance.[15] Since FY2007, there has been a looming shortfall in the IWTF. In recent years Congress has taken measures to ensure temporary solvency of the IWTF, either by appropriating federal funds beyond the aforementioned 50% federal requirement (FY2009 and FY2010), or by limiting IWTF expenditures to the amount available under current year fuel tax revenues (FY2011-FY2013). The IWTF is expected to have a balance of approximately $70 million at the end of FY2013. Without changes to the current system, needed funding for eligible work is expected to continue to exceed available funding.

In the past multiple Administrations have proposed fees (e.g., lock user fees, congestion fees) that would have increased IWTF revenues. These fees have been opposed by users and rejected by Congress. In 2011, users endorsed a plan of their own that would increase the current fuel tax by $0.06-$0.08 per gallon and alter the cost-share arrangement for some IWTF projects to increase the portion paid for by the federal government. H.R. 1149 would authorize this proposal, which has been opposed by the Obama Administration.

Recent estimates by the Corps indicate that one project, Olmsted Lock and Dam on the Ohio River, is expected to use up the majority of IWTF revenues over the next 10 years.[16] At the same time, other navigation construction and major rehabilitation work is expected to stall. Without a new source of revenue or some other change directed by Congress, the overall number of inland waterway projects is expected to be extremely limited. Changes to IWTF policies have historically been under the jurisdiction of the authorizing committees, but in recent years appropriators have expressed frustration with the lack of action on this issue.

In FY2014, the Administration requested limited appropriations for IWTF projects based on current-year fuel tax revenues.[17] This is the same approach that was proposed and enacted in FY2011-FY2013. The FY2014 Administration budget requested approximately $94 million in inland waterway spending from the IWTF, with an equal amount to be drawn from the General Fund of the Treasury. The Administration also assumed an additional $80 million in new revenues from an unspecified user fee, presumably separate from the current fuel tax. The majority of FY2014 requested IWTF funds were proposed for the Olmsted Project. The House Appropriations Committee disagreed with the user fee approach, but continued to agree with the approach of limiting appropriations to current year fuel revenue. The Senate Appropriations

---

[14] For more information on inland waterways, see CRS Report R41430, *Inland Waterways: Recent Proposals and Issues for Congress*, by Charles V. Stern.

[15] Pursuant to the Water Resources Development Act of 1986 (P.L. 99-662), the fuel tax has been fixed at $0.20 per gallon since 1992.

[16] Currently the Olmsted Project accounts for almost all IWTF appropriations. The project was originally authorized at a cost of $775 million (plus inflationary increases) but recently required an increase to its authorization ceiling in accordance with Section 902(b) of the Water Resources Development Act of 1986 (33 U.S.C. §2280).The FY2014 Continuing Appropriations Act, P.L. 113-46, increased the project's authorization from $775 million to $2.92 billion.

[17] Assuming annual fuel tax revenues of approximately $95 million, spending on inland waterways construction for FY2014 would be approximately $190 million for each year (or approximately $60 million less than the average funding provided from FY1992-2010).

Committee also disagreed with the user fee proposal, and proposed exempting the Olmsted Project from IWTF cost sharing requirements in FY2014. This would allow other IWTF projects to proceed using the trust fund revenues, but would fund Olmsted entirely out of the General Fund of the Treasury.

For more information on inland waterways, see CRS Report R41430, *Inland Waterways: Recent Proposals and Issues for Congress*, by Charles V. Stern.

Ecosystem Restoration Projects

The Corps portion of the Energy and Water bill typically includes funding for ecosystem restoration projects, such as restoration of the Everglades in South Florida.[18] Previously some in Congress have criticized the fact that while the Corps has requested reductions for some "traditional" activities in recent budgets, funding for Corps environmental business line activities, which include ecosystem restoration projects, has largely remained the same. For FY2014, the Administration requested $449 million (approximately 9% of the total FY2014 Corps request, spread among several accounts) for ecosystem restoration projects. This amount is less than has been appropriated for these activities in recent years. Everglades restoration was among the ecosystem restoration projects proposed for reduction in the FY2014 request. The President's budget requested $88 million for Everglades restoration, or a significant reduction from the FY2012 enacted level of $135 million. The House Appropriations Committee recommended $83.6 million for the project, and the Senate Appropriations Committee agreed with the Administration's request.

Continuing Authorities Program

Projects funded under the Corps' Continuing Authorities Programs (CAPs) are typically smaller projects that can be carried out without obtaining a project-specific study or construction authorization or project-specific appropriations.[19] CAPs are referred to by the section number in the bill where the CAP was first authorized. The Administration's FY2014 budget requested $29 million in funding for five of the nine CAPs, or a significant decrease from previous enacted levels.[20] The Administration proposed no funding for four CAPs, including Section 14 (emergency streambank and shoreline protection), Section 103 (shore protection), Section 107 (navigation), and Section 208 (snagging and clearing for flood control). The House Appropriations Committee proposed $33 million in funding for eight CAPs, while the Senate Appropriations Committee recommended $50 million in funding for eight CAPs.

---

[18] Along with the Department of the Interior, the Corps typically receives funding for the Comprehensive Everglades Restoration Program, or CERP. For more information regarding Everglades restoration funding, see CRS Report R42007, *Everglades Restoration: Federal Funding and Implementation Progress*, by Charles V. Stern.

[19] A summary of projects under the Continuing Authorities Program is provided on p. 11 of CRS Report R41243, *Army Corps of Engineers: Water Resource Authorizations, Appropriations, and Activities*, by Nicole T. Carter and Charles V. Stern.

[20] The FY2012 enacted total for these programs was $43 million.

Title II: Department of the Interior[21]

Bureau of Reclamation and Central Utah Project

The Energy and Water Development bill includes funding for two agencies within the Department of the Interior: the Bureau of Reclamation and the Central Utah Project (CUP). The total discretionary FY2014 budget request for Title II funding for Reclamation and CUP was $1.049 billion. The House-passed bill recommended $964.8 million for these programs, and the Senate recommended approximately $1.099 billion.

Reclamation has released an operating plan for FY2013 that accounts for sequestration's effect on FY2013 enacted level under the BCA and ATRA and allows for comparison to FY2014 proposed spending levels.[22] While the overall appropriation for Reclamation and CUP for FY2013 was $1.066 billion, Reclamation's estimate of actual funding for both agencies under the FY2013 operating plan (i.e., after the sequester and other reductions) was $1.014 billion.[23]

The FY2014 request for the Bureau of Reclamation and CUP included an "offset" of $53.2 million for the Central Valley Project (CVP) Restoration Fund (Congress does not list this line item as an offset), yielding a "net" discretionary authority of $996 million.[24] As in previous years, additional funding is estimated to be available for FY2014 via "permanent and other" funds, but these funds are not included in net discretionary totals.

Table 5. Energy and Water Development Appropriations
Title II: Central Utah Project Completion Account

($ millions)

Program	FY2012 Approp.	FY2013 Approp.	FY2014 Request	House	Senate	Conf.
Central Utah Water Conservancy District	26.7	19.8	—	7.7	—	
Mitigation and Conservation Commission Activities	2.0	1.2	—	1.0	—	
Total, Central Utah Project	**28.7**	**21.0**	—	**8.7**	—	

Source: FY2014 budget request, H.Rept. 113-35, S.Rept. 113-47.

Notes: The FY2014 budget request proposed to transfer the Central Utah Project Completion Account to the Bureau of Reclamation. See Table 6 below for Administration and Senate recommendations for this account.

---

[21] This section was prepared by Charles V. Stern.

[22] The operating plan is available at http://www.usbr.gov/budget/.

[23] Unless otherwise indicated, all references to FY2013 amounts in this section are to FY2013 appropriated amounts before taking into account the BCA and ATRA.

[24] This offset is consistent with prior year appropriations.

Table 6. Energy and Water Development Appropriations
Title II: Bureau of Reclamation

($ millions)

Program	FY2012 Approp.	FY2013 Approp.	FY2014 Request	House	Senate	Conf.
Water and Related Resources	895.0	893.2	791.1	812.7	945.8	
Policy and Administration	60.0	59.9	60.0	60.0	60.0	
CVP Restoration Fund (CVPRF)	53.1	53.0	53.3	53.3	53.3	
Calif. Bay-Delta (CALFED)	39.7	39.6	37.0	30.0	37.0	
San Joaquin Restoration Fund[a]	—	—	26.0	—	—	
Indian Water Rights Settlement[a]	—	—	78.7	—	—	
Central Utah Project Completion[b]	—	—	3.5	—	3.5	
Gross Current Reclamation Authority	**1,047.7**	**1,045.7**	**1,049.6**	**956.0**	**1,099.6**	
Total, Title II Current Authority (CUP and Reclamation)	**1,076.4**	**1,066.7**	**1,049.6**	**964.8**	**1,099.6**	

Source: FY2014 budget request and FY2013 Bureau of Reclamation Work Plan.

Notes: FY2013 enacted level does not include sequester and other related reductions. Totals may not add due to rounding.

a. As in previous requests, the Administration's request includes funding for these items, which have in the past been funded within Water and Related Resources, as new accounts.

b. The Administration proposed to transfer the Central Utah Project Completion Account to the Bureau of Reclamation. To date, this proposal has not been enacted. See Table 5 above for House amounts, which were not provided as an account under Reclamation.

Central Utah Project

The Obama Administration requested $3.5 million for the Central Utah Project (CUP) Completion Account in FY2014, or $17.5 million less than the FY2013 enacted amount. Significantly, in FY2014 the Administration once again proposed to make Reclamation responsible for oversight and implementation of CUP (these responsibilities are currently housed within a separate office in DOI). The Senate Appropriations Committee agreed with the President's request, but in its bill the House retained CUP as a separate account and provided $8.7 million for this project.

Bureau of Reclamation

Most of the large dams and water diversion structures in the West were built by, or with the assistance of, the Bureau of Reclamation. Whereas the Army Corps of Engineers built hundreds of flood control and navigation projects, Reclamation's mission was to develop water supplies, primarily for irrigation to reclaim arid lands in the West. Today, Reclamation manages hundreds of dams and diversion projects, including more than 300 storage reservoirs in 17 western states. These projects provide water to approximately 10 million acres of farmland and a population of 31 million. Reclamation is the largest wholesale supplier of water in the 17 western states and the second-largest hydroelectric power producer in the nation. Reclamation facilities also provide substantial flood control, recreation, and fish and wildlife benefits. Operations of Reclamation facilities are often controversial, particularly for their effect on fish and wildlife species and conflicts among competing water users.

As with the Corps of Engineers, the Reclamation budget is made up largely of individual project funding lines and relatively few "programs." Also similar to the Corps, previously these Reclamation projects have often been subject to earmark disclosure rules. The current moratorium on earmarks affects Congress's ability to steer money toward specific Reclamation projects, as it has done in the past.

Reclamation's single largest account, Water and Related Resources, encompasses the agency's traditional programs and projects, including construction, operations and maintenance, dam safety, and ecosystem restoration, among others. The Obama Administration requested $791 million for the Water and Related Resources account for FY2014, or a decrease from the FY2013 enacted amount. Most of this decrease was due to shifting of funds to new accounts for Indian water rights settlements and San Joaquin restoration. The House-passed bill provided $812 million for Water and Related Resources, and the Senate Appropriations Committee provided $946 million for this account in its recommendation. Neither the House nor the Senate included the Administration's proposed new accounts for Indian water rights funding (although some of this funding was provided within Water and Related Resources).

Central Valley Project (CVP) Operations

The CVP in California is one of Reclamation's largest and most complex water projects, and limited deliveries to CVP contractors are often the subject of appropriations and authorization debates. In recent years, Reclamation has had to limit water deliveries and pumping from CVP facilities due to drought and other factors, including environmental restrictions. In previous appropriations bills, this action has resulted in attempts to prevent Reclamation from implementing Biological Opinions (BiOps), some of which restrict CVP operations because of the project's potential effects on certain fish species.[25] Previous proposals to restrict implementation of BiOps in the CVP, including amendments to appropriations bills, have not been enacted. However, other measures to lessen the impact of these restrictions have been enacted, and related legislation is currently under consideration.[26]

---

[25] The two BiOps in question have found that continued operation of the projects under a plan developed and implemented in 2004 (known as the Operations Criteria and Plan, or OCAP) would jeopardize the existence of delta smelt and salmon and other endangered species in California. OCAP allowed increased pumping from the delta, which some believe has further imperiled fish species listed as threatened or endangered under the Endangered Species Act. Others note that factors such as invasive species, pollution, and non-federal withdrawals of water from the delta have contributed to fishery declines. Critically low numbers of delta smelt resulted in a court-imposed limit on pumping at certain times. These and other restrictions have led to low water deliveries for certain water districts (e.g., those with junior water rights).

[26] Most prominently, H.R. 1837 in the 112th Congress would have, among other things, altered the current regime for water deliveries in the Central Valley and repealed the San Joaquin River Restoration Act. For more information, see CRS Report R42375, *H.R. 1837—The Sacramento-San Joaquin Valley Water Reliability Act*, by Betsy A. Cody.

San Joaquin River Restoration Fund

The San Joaquin River Restoration Fund was authorized by the enactment of Title X of the Omnibus Public Land Management Act of 2009 (P.L. 111-11), the San Joaquin River Restoration Settlement Act. The Fund is to be used to implement fisheries restoration and water management provisions of a stipulated settlement agreement for the *Natural Resources Defense Council et al. v. Rodgers* lawsuit.[27] The Fund is supported through the combination of a reallocation of Central Valley Project Restoration Fund receipts from the Friant Division water users and accelerated payment of Friant water users' capital repayment obligations, as well as other federal and non-federal sources. The Settlement Act provided $88 million from the Restoration Fund to be available without further appropriation. In recent years, some have proposed repealing the settlement outright.[28]

Reclamation reports that in FY2014, the balance of the aforementioned mandatory appropriations is expected to be exhausted. Separately, Reclamation has also proposed an allocation of $26 million in discretionary funding for FY2014 within a new account for San Joaquin River restoration activities. The House Appropriations Committee provided no funding for these activities. The Senate Appropriations Committee disagreed with the Administration's request of funding for these activities in a separate account, but provided $26 million in funding for San Joaquin River restoration as a line item under the Friant Division of the Central Valley Project in the Water and Related Resources account.

WaterSMART Program

In recent years Reclamation has combined funding for several individual "bureau-wide" programs that promote water conservation into a single program—the WaterSMART (Sustain and Manage America's Resources for Tomorrow) Program. The program is part of an effort by the Department of the Interior to focus on water conservation, re-use, and planning. In the FY2013 request the WaterSMART program included five components: WaterSMART Grants, Basin Studies, Title XVI Projects, the Cooperative Watershed Management Program, and Water Conservation Field Services.[29] The FY2014 President's budget request for all WaterSMART programs was $35.4 million. The House bill recommended eliminating funding for WaterSMART Grants and Basin Studies. The Senate Appropriations Committee recommended an increase of $8 million for WaterSMART grants and otherwise agreed with the Administration's request. Funding levels for WaterSMART programs are shown in **Table 7**.

---

[27] Construction of Friant Dam in the 1940s and subsequent diversion of San Joaquin River water to off-stream agricultural uses blocked salmon migration and dewatered stretches of the San Joaquin, resulting in elimination of spring-run Chinook into the upper reaches of the river. One goal of the settlement is to bring back the salmon run; another is to reduce or avoid adverse water supply impacts to Friant Division long-term contractors. For more information on the settlement agreement and the San Joaquin River Restoration Fund, see CRS Report R40125, *Title X of H.R. 146: San Joaquin River Restoration*, by Betsy A. Cody and Pervaze A. Sheikh.

[28] See footnote 26.

[29] Prior to FY2012, the Water Conservation Field Services program and the Cooperative Watershed Management Program had been a "bureau-wide" program. For consistency, comparisons to prior year funding in this report include this program within WaterSMART totals.

Table 7. Reclamation WaterSMART Program

(selected programs, $ millions)

Program Name	FY2012 Approp.	FY2013 Approp.	FY2014 Request	House	Senate	Conf.
WaterSMART Grants	12.2	22.6	12.0	—	20.0	
Basin Studies	4.9	6.0	4.7	—	4.7	
Title XVI Projects	24.7	20.0	14.0	13.3	22.0	
Cooperative Watershed Management Program	0.25	0.25	0.25	0.24	0.25	
Water Conservation Field Services	5.0	6.2	3.4	3.01	3.4	
Total	**47.1**	**52.0**	**35.4**	**16.5**	**50.39**	

Source: Bureau of Reclamation FY2014 Congressional Justifications, FY2013 Reclamation Work Plan.

Title III: Department of Energy

The Energy and Water Development bill has funded all DOE's programs since FY2005. Major DOE activities funded by the Energy and Water bill include research and development on renewable energy and energy efficiency, nuclear power, fossil energy R&D, the Strategic Petroleum Reserve, energy statistics, general science, environmental cleanup, and nuclear weapons programs.

The FY2012 appropriations act, P.L. 112-74, funded DOE programs at $26.4 billion. The FY2013 continuing resolution, P.L. 113-6, funded DOE programs at the FY2012 level, with some exceptions, and subject to the sequestration requirements of the Budget Control Act that went into effect March 1, 2013. The Administration's request for DOE programs for FY2014 totaled $28.9 billion. H.R. 2609, as passed by the House July 10, 2013, totaled $24.9 billion for DOE programs. S. 1245, as reported out by the Senate Appropriations Committee June 27, would fund DOE programs at $28.2 billion.

Table 8. Energy and Water Development Appropriations
Title III: Department of Energy

($ millions)

Program	FY2012 Approp.	FY2013 Approp.[a]	FY2014 Request	House	Senate
ENERGY PROGRAMS					
Energy Efficiency and Renewable Energy	1,780.5	1,810.5	2,775.7	958.0	2,280.0
Electricity Delivery and Energy Reliability	136.2	139.2	169.0	0.0[b]	149.0
Nuclear Energy	760.5	757.5	735.5	656.4	735.5
Race to the Top	0.0	0.0	200.0	0.0	0.0
Fossil Energy R&D	337.1	532.9	420.6	430.0	420.6
Naval Petrol. and Oil Shale Reserves	14.9	14.9	20.0	14.9	20.0
Strategic Petroleum Reserve	192.7	192.3	189.4	189.4	189.4
Northeast Home Heating Oil Reserve	10.1	4.1	8.0	8.0	8.0
Energy Information Administration	105.0	104.8	117.0	100.0	117.0
Non-Defense Environmental Cleanup	235.3	235.3	213.0	213.0	233.0
Uranium D&D Fund	472.2	472.0	554.8	545.0	554.9
Science	4,935.0	4,866.2	5,152.8	4,653.0	5,152.8
Energy Transformation Acceleration Fund (ARPA-E)	275.0	264.5	379.0	70.0	379.0
Nuclear Waste Disposal	0.0	0.0	0.0	0.0	0.0
Departmental Admin. (net)	126.0	125.7	118.4	13.0	126.4
Office of Inspector General	42.0	41.9	42.1	42.0	42.1
Adv. Tech. Vehicles Manuf. Loan	6.0	6.0	6.0	6.0	6.0
Sec. 1705 Loan Guarantee	0.0	0.0	26.0	0.0	20.0
TOTAL, ENERGY PROGRAMS	**9,428.5**	**9,567.8**	**11,101.2**	**7,898.7**	**10,434.5**
DEFENSE ACTIVITIES					
National Nuclear Security Administration (NNSA)					
Weapons Activities	7,214.8	7,574.9	7,868.4	7,675.0	7,868.4
Nuclear Nonproliferation	2,301.0	2,344.5	2,140.1	2,100.0	2,180.1
Naval Reactors	1,080.0	1,079.7	1,246.1	1,109.0	1,312.1
Office of Administrator	410.0	409.9	397.8	373.0	397.8
Total, NNSA	**11,005.8**	**11,498.0**	**11,652.5**	**11,257.0**	**11,758.5**
Defense Environmental Cleanup	5,003.0	5,013.0	5,316.9	4,773.0	5,146.5
Other Defense Activities	823.4	821.7	749.1	830.0	762.1
Defense Nuclear Waste Disposal	0.0	0.0	0.0	0.0	0.0

Program	FY2012 Approp.	FY2013 Approp.ᵃ	FY2014 Request	House	Senate
TOTAL, DEFENSE ACTIVITIES	16,832.0	17,332.6	17,718.5	16,860.0	17,667.1
POWER MARKETING ADMINISTRATION (PMAs)					
Southeastern	0.0		0.0	0.0	0.0
Southwestern	11.9	11.9	11.9	11.9	11.9
Western	96.0	133.9	95.9	95.9	95.9
Falcon & Amistad O&M	0.2	0.2	0.4	0.4	0.4
TOTAL, PMAs	108.1	146.0	108.2	108.2	108.2
Total, Title III	26,368.6	27,046.4	28,927.9	24,866.9	28,209.9

Source: FY2014 budget request; H.Rept. 113-135; S.Rept. 113-47.

a. Source: S.Rept. 113-47. Figures do not reflect the March 1, 2013, sequester of funds under P.L. 112-25.

b. The House bill would merge EDER programs with EERE. H.Rept. 112-135 did not specify a particular funding level for EDER.

Key Policy Issues—Department of Energy

DOE administers a wide variety of programs with different functions and missions. In the following pages, some of the most important programs are described and major issues are identified, in approximately the order in which they appear in **Table 8**.

Energy Efficiency and Renewable Energy (EERE)[30]

President Obama has declared energy efficiency and renewable energy to be a high priority, stressing their importance to jobs, economic growth, and U.S. manufacturing competitiveness. For example, the 2013 *Economic Report of the President* notes that "President Obama has set a goal of once again doubling generation from wind, solar, and geothermal sources by 2020." But Congress so far hasn't supported his efforts to boost spending for these programs. His proposed FY2011 budget for EERE of $2.4 billion was reduced to $1.8 billion, and his FY2012 proposal of $3.2 billion was cut to $1.8 billion.

For FY2014, DOE requests $2.78 billion for the EERE programs. Compared with the FY2013 appropriation, the FY2014 request would increase EERE funding by about $979 million, or more than 50%.

DOE requests an additional $169 million for Electricity Delivery and Energy Reliability (EDER) programs. **Table 9** gives the programmatic breakdown for EERE and EDER.

---

[30] This section was prepared by Fred Sissine.

Table 9. Energy Efficiency and Renewable Energy Programs

($ millions)

Program	FY2012 Approp.	FY2013 Approp.[a]	FY2014 Request	House	Senate	Conf.
Hydrogen/Fuel Cell Technologies	101.3	103.4	100.0	65.0	100.0	
Biomass and Biorefinery Systems	195.0	198.8	282.0	120.0	245.0	
Solar Energy	284.7	288.3	356.5	65.3	310.0	
—Concentrating Solar Power (CSP)	44.9	—	90.1	—	—	
—Photovoltaic (PV) Power	75.6	—	79.1	—	—	
Wind Energy	91.8	93.0	144.0	24.0	110.0	
Geothermal Technology	37.0	37.8	60.0	12.0	60.0	
Water Power (Hydro/Ocean)	58.1	58.6	55.0	24.0	59.0	
Subtotal, Renewable and Hydrogen	767.9	779.9	997.5	310.3	884.0	
Vehicle Technologies	321.0	328.0	575.0	205.0	415.0	
Building Technologies	214.7	218.7	300.0	65.3	230.0	
Advanced Manufacturing	112.7	115.3	365.0	120.0	216.0	
Federal Energy Management	29.9	—	36.0	0.0	30.0	
Subtotal, Efficiency R&D	678.3	—	1,276.0	390.3	891.0	
Facilities and Infrastructure	26.3	26.2	46.0	31.0	46.0	
Program Direction	165.0	—	185.0	—	185.0	
Strategic Programs	25.0	24.9	36.0	2.0	28.0	
R&D Subtotal	1,662.5	—	2,540.5	810.5	2,034.0	
Renewables Deployment	10.0	9.9	7.0	3.0	10.0	
Subtotal, Demonstration and Deployment	10.0	9.9	7.0	3.0	10.0	
Weatherization Grants	68.0	67.6	184.0	77.1	184.0	
State Energy Grants	50.0	49.7	57.0	12.0	53.0	
Use of Prior Year Balances	-9.9	-10.0	-12.8	0.0	0.0	
Total EERE Appropriation	1,780.5	1,796.6	2,775.7	902.6	2,281.0	
Electricity Delivery and Energy Reliability (EDER)	136.2	—	169.0	—	149.0	

Sources: FY2014 budget request; H.Rept. 113-135; S.Rept. 113-47.

a. Estimates of the FY2013 enacted levels are taken from H.Rept. 113-135. Those amounts do not reflect the 251A sequester. Also excluded is the House report recommendation for $157 million in rescissions of prior-year unobligated balances.

EERE Active Project Management

The request emphasizes that the current fiscal and budget constraints make it important that EERE use funds as efficiently and carefully as possible. Thus, starting in FY2014, EERE states that it will fully and uniformly implement a regimen of Active Project Management. Under this regimen, every competitive project awarded will take the form of a cooperative agreement, not a grant. This, says DOE, would enable greater EERE oversight. Also, each project would be subject to aggressive, annual go/no-go milestones, rigorous quarterly reviews, and early termination in the event of insufficient technical performance. DOE says that this approach would ensure that EERE has the correct tools and project oversight to maximize the taxpayer's return on investment.

EERE-wide Cross-Cutting Initiatives

The request emphasizes five broad initiatives that cut across multiple EERE programs:

(1) Grid Integration Initiative. Under this initiative, launched in 2012, EERE's vehicles, solar, and buildings programs will work in coordination with DOE's Grid Tech Team[31] to address electric grid integration barriers and opportunities associated with variable, distributed renewable energy generators, electric vehicle charging, and building efficiency and controls. EERE will coordinate with DOE's Office of Electricity Delivery and Energy Reliability (EDER). EERE would issue an $80 million project announcement, jointly funded by three programs: Solar ($30 million), Vehicles ($20 million), and Buildings ($30 million).

(2) EV Everywhere Grand Challenge. This DOE-wide initiative aims to make technology breakthroughs that would enable the United States, by 2022, to become the first country in the world to invent and produce plug-in electric vehicles that are as affordable and convenient as gasoline-powered vehicles.

(3) SunShot Grand Challenge. This DOE-wide initiative seeks to achieve directly cost-competitive solar power by 2020.

(4) Clean Energy Manufacturing Initiative. This new EERE initiative would aim to dramatically improve U.S. competitiveness in the manufacture of clean energy products (like solar modules, LEDs, batteries, and wind blades) and to strengthen U.S. competitiveness across multiple manufacturing industries through increased energy productivity.

(5) Wide Bandgap Semiconductors for Clean Energy Initiative. Wide bandgap semiconductor technology was initially developed for military and solid-state lighting uses. DOE believes it is a key next-generation platform for semiconductor devices with the potential for developing high-power-conversion electronics that are much more compact, more energy efficient, and able to operate at much higher temperatures and voltages. DOE finds that this "revolutionary" technology could be a platform for the next generation of electric drivetrains, solar inverters, high-efficiency motors, solid-state transformers for the grid, and many other critical, clean energy applications.

---

[31] DOE created the Grid Tech Team to develop a stronger and more extensive network of effective public-private partnerships needed to ease the transition to a more modern grid. DOE, EDER, *DOE Grid Tech Team*, http://energy.gov/oe/services/doe-grid-tech-team.

House Appropriations Committee Recommendation

Expressing concern about controlling budget expenses—and citing a need to focus EERE programs on efforts to curb gasoline and electricity prices—the committee recommends cutting overall EERE funding relative to the FY2013 level by half. Further, the committee report proposes to merge EERE with the Office of Electricity Delivery and Energy Reliability (EDER). The report also contains several management and program directives, which are noted below, in the context of specific program areas.

Senate Appropriation Committee Recommendation

Urging EERE to apply more funding to near-term commercialization efforts in partnership with the private sector, the committee recommends FY2014 funding at a level just slightly higher than the request.

Hydrogen/Fuel Cell Program

This program aims to reduce petroleum use, greenhouse gas emissions, and criteria air pollutants, while contributing to a more diverse and efficient energy infrastructure. The program supports applied research, development, and demonstration (RD&D) of hydrogen and fuel cell technologies, as well as efforts to overcome economic and institutional barriers to commercial deployment. DOE requests $100 million—a bit below the FY2013 estimate—seeking to increase hydrogen R&D and manufacturing R&D slightly, while reducing fuel cell R&D slightly. The House bill proposes a one-third cut below FY2013 to $65 million, while the Senate bill would provide the full requested amount of $100 million.

Biomass and Biorefinery Program Initiatives

This program aims to foster a domestic bioenergy industry that produces renewable biofuels, bioproducts, and biopower. The goals are to curb oil dependence, reduce greenhouse gas emissions, and stimulate economic and job development—especially in the farms and forests of rural areas. While biofuels and industrial bioproducts (plastics, solvents, alcohols) may soon be price-competitive, swings in oil prices pose an ongoing challenge to achieve cost-competitiveness. The program strategy addresses a feedstock collection barrier by focusing on converting raw biomass to solid pellets or to "green crude" bio-oil that is easy to transport at large scale.

Recent goals expand the program scope to include the development of biofuels that will contribute to production targets of the Renewable Fuel Standard (RFS). These "drop-in" liquid fuels are largely compatible with existing infrastructure to deliver, blend, and dispense fuels. Examples include biomass-based hydrocarbon fuels (renewable gasoline, diesel, and jet fuel), hydrocarbons from algae, and biobutanol. The program aims to help the non-food "drop-in" biofuels (renewable gasoline, diesel, and jet fuel) reach a wholesale finished-fuel cost under $3 per gasoline gallon-equivalent (gge) by 2017.

DOE requests $282 million in FY2014 for Bioenergy (Biomass and Biorefinery) programs, an $83 million increase over the $199 million estimate for FY2013. The largest requested subprogram increase would go to conversion technologies. That increase would include $20 million for the low cost carbon fiber initiative. Another large increase would go to the integrated biorefineries subprogram. That increase would include $45 million (justified under the Defense Production Act) to support commercial demonstration-scale, military-grade fuel production from biomass through DOE collaboration with the U.S. Department of Agriculture (USDA). This would be partially offset by a $14 million cut for algae and advanced feedstocks.

The House bill recommends about 60% of the FY2013 estimate, while the Senate proposes about 23% more than FY2013.

Solar Energy

For the Solar Program, DOE requests $356 million, an increase of $68 million over FY2013 estimate. The concentrating solar power (CSP) subprogram would increase by $45 million, mainly for work on thermal storage to improve grid integration. The balance of systems subprogram would grow by $29 million to enable work with state and local governments to reduce permitting, interconnection, inspection, and other soft costs. Funding for the systems integration subprogram would rise by $16 million, focused mainly on power electronics and other means to improve integration of solar power with the grid. Those increases would be partially offset by a $34 million cut to the innovations in manufacturing competitiveness subprogram. The House bill recommends a cut of $223 million (77%) from the FY2013 estimate, while the Senate bill proposes an increase of 22 million (8%) over FY2013.

Wind Energy

For the Wind Program, DOE requests a $51 million increase over the FY2013 estimate. Half of that increase, $26 million, would go to the technology development and testing subprogram, mainly for wind power plant optimization modeling. That increase would support analysis of new technology, advanced manufacturing, and a technology incubator. Funding for offshore wind would grow by $12 million. Also, the technology application subprogram would increase by $17 million. That increase would cover resource characterization to better assess wind plant capacity factor performance, activities to optimize grid integration, and analysis of market barriers arising from impacts on radar and birds and from environmental impacts of the first installed offshore projects. The House bill recommends a cut of $69 million (74%) from the FY2013 estimate, while the Senate bill proposes an increase of 17 million (18%) over FY2013.

Geothermal Technologies

The program aims to lower the risk of resource exploration and cut power production costs to six cents/kilowatt-hour (kwh) for hydrothermal power by 2020 and for newly developed technologies by 2030. For the Geothermal Program, DOE requests $60 million, an increase of $22 million over FY2013. Enhanced Geothermal Systems (EGS) would get an increase of $26 million to establish a field lab and to support strategic R&D. This increase would be partially offset by a $3 million cut for activities involving low temperature co-produced resources. The House bill recommends a $26 million (68%) cut from the FY2013 estimate, while the Senate bill proposes an increase of $22 million over FY2013.

Water Power

Water power technologies employ marine and hydrokinetic (wave, tidal, current, and ocean thermal) resources—and conventional hydropower resources—to generate electricity. Hydropower technology is well established, but the fledgling industry for marine and hydrokinetic (MHK) power facilities is still looking to develop a clear technology theme. For the Water Power Program, DOE requests $55 million, a cut of $4 million below FY2013.The budget request would add $6 million for MHK RD&D, demonstration infrastructure development, and light-weight materials in manufacturing. Hydropower funding would be cut by $9 million. The House bill recommends a $35 million (59%) cut from the FY2013 estimate, while the Senate bill proposes to maintain the FY2013 level.

Vehicle Technologies

This program is driven by the 10-year EV-Everywhere Challenge (launched in 2012), which aims to achieve parity for plug-in electric vehicle (EV) affordability and convenience by 2022. The EV Challenge focuses on advanced battery technology, power electronics, and advanced charging technology—with the goal of assuring U.S. leadership in the global market for next generation electric vehicle technology. A key supporting technology goal is to cut 2008 battery production cost 70% by 2015 (and 88% by 2022). Further, the program seeks to achieve: (1) a cut of 1.8 million barrels per day (16%) in the national oil use trend by 2020, (2) a fuel economy of 62 miles per gallon (mpg) for cars by 2025, and (3) a 50% increase in heavy duty truck fuel economy by 2015. Also, the program participates in the Grid Integration Initiative.

To help achieve those goals and support the EV Everywhere initiative, DOE seeks the largest EERE FY2014 program increase—$247 million over the estimate for FY2013. The subprogram on batteries and electric drives would increase by $122 million, including a $71 million increase for battery cost reduction through innovative manufacturing R&D, scale-up of advanced battery component materials, and next-generation "beyond lithium" research. A $36 million increase would go to advanced power electronics R&D (on wide bandgap semiconductors) to support higher performance electric drive systems. Under the materials subprogram, R&D on lightweight materials (carbon fiber composites, aluminum parts, magnesium alloys) would grow by $22 million to support the EV Everywhere initiative.

The deployment subprogram would get an increase of $90 million for a new initiative to establish "Alternative Fuel Vehicle Community Partner Projects." Competitive (and cost-shared) awards (up to 9 awards of $10 million each) would be made for state and local community-based projects that would last three to four years. The objective would be the creation of replicable "model communities" that develop policies, procedures, and infrastructure to successfully displace on-road vehicle petroleum use with alternatives such as natural gas, electricity (e.g., plug-in EVs), or biofuels.

The House bill recommends a $123 million (38%) cut from the FY2013 estimate, while the Senate bill proposes an increase of $87 million (27%) over FY2013.

Building Technologies

This program develops energy efficiency measures to curb building-related energy costs, with a goal of reducing energy use 50% by 2030. The program strategy is designed with three linked paths: improve building components (envelope/windows, HVAC, lighting, and sensors/controls), strengthen market pull (through cooperation with private industry), and raise energy efficiency levels for new equipment (via standards) and new buildings (via model codes).

DOE requests $300 million for FY2014, an increase of $81 million over the FY2013 estimate. Most of the requested increase, $71 million, would go to the emerging technologies subprogram. From that amount, $41 million would support competitive (and cost-shared) demonstration projects to accelerate commercialization of technologies that are within three years or less of market-readiness. Specific areas include advanced building controls and "next generation" air conditioning technologies. Also, $30 million requested for the Grid Integration Initiative would address R&D on how building energy control systems transact (provide status, availability, identity) with each other and with the electric grid. Projects would likely cover predictive data analytics, sensors, and energy control systems.

The request also seeks $24 million for another year of funding for the Building Energy Efficiency Innovation Hub. Additionally, $15 million of the increase would support EERE efforts to accelerate the development of energy efficiency equipment standards and building codes.

The House bill recommends a $153 million (70%) cut from the FY2013 estimate, while the Senate bill proposes an increase of $11 million (5%) over FY2013.

Advanced Manufacturing

Domestic manufacturers face increasing challenges in the global marketplace. The Advanced Manufacturing Office (AMO) was designed to focus on national interests—especially concerns about jobs, critical materials, and international competitiveness. The general goal for AMO programs is to reduce the energy use of manufactured goods across targeted product life-cycles by 50% over 10 years. More specific objectives include (1) 50% energy savings through advanced materials and industrial processes, (2) help leading companies cut energy intensity by 25% over 10 years, and (3) facilitate installation of 40 GW (million kilowatts) of combined heat and power equipment by 2020.[32]

To meet the above-noted goals and objectives DOE requests $365 million, a net increase of $250 million over the FY2013 estimate. Most of the requested increase ($183 million) would go to the subprogram on Advanced Manufacturing R&D Facilities, with the remainder split between Next Generation Manufacturing R&D Projects ($60 million) and Industrial Technical Assistance ($10 million).

The proposed $183 million increase for Advanced R&D Facilities would include $177 million more for clean energy manufacturing R&D facilities. That additional funding would allow the program to support the creation of at least three new Clean Energy Manufacturing Innovation (CEMI) Institutes, consistent with the President's vision for a larger, multi-agency National Network for Manufacturing Innovation (NNMI).[33]

---

[32] DOE, EERE-Advanced Manufacturing Office, *FY14 Budget At-a-Glance*, http://www1.eere.energy.gov/office_eere/pdfs/budget/manufacturing_ataglance_2014.pdf.

[33] The NNMI model was designed to induce collaboration and spread risk, complement university research, and focus national manufacturing policy. For more about NNMI, see http://manufacturing.gov/nnmi.html and http://www.manufacturing.gov/docs/nnmi_prelim_design.pdf.

CEMI is a new cross-cutting activity that would be anchored by AMO and would incorporate activities under many of EERE's other programs.[34] The main goal is to improve U.S. competitiveness in the manufacturing of clean energy products, such as solar photovoltaic modules, LEDs, batteries, and wind turbine blades. The CEMI institutes would provide small- and medium-sized enterprises affordable access to cutting-edge physical and virtual manufacturing capabilities (e.g., 3-D printing equipment) and facilitate technology use in the U.S. manufacturing sector to bolster its global competitiveness. DOE plans to invest $70 million-$120 million into each CEMI institute, to be used over a five- to seven-year period. For each institute, DOE plans to provide up-front funding to the greatest extent possible.

Another R&D facility, the Critical Materials Hub, was created in FY2012 to focus on technologies that enable manufacturers to make better use of critical materials (e.g., rare earth elements) and to eliminate the need for materials that are vulnerable to supply disruptions. Many rare earth elements are essential to technologies of the clean energy industry.[35] Examples include wind turbines, solar photovoltaic panels, electric vehicles, and energy-efficient lighting. DOE seeks to extend the Hub's operation for a third year by requesting $25 million, a $5 million increase over FY2012.

Under the Next Generation Manufacturing Projects subprogram, advanced R&D projects focus on technology areas with the greatest potential impact on clean energy manufacturing and energy productivity-related competitiveness. DOE requests an increase of $60 million over FY2012. The increase would support at least three new project competitions—in specific technology areas—of about $20 million to $40 million each. Previously identified and approved technology areas include additive manufacturing (3-D printing), wide bandgap semiconductors (efficient power conversion), low-cost carbon fiber (lightweight) materials, and other technologies that would benefit multiple clean energy sectors. Also, one of the three competitions would be established as an "incubator activity" project. It would get up to $20 million in support for a new technology area that might not be included among the above-referenced list of approved technology areas.

For Industrial Technical Assistance, the requested $10 million increase would expand combined heat & power (CHP) partnerships to provide greater technical assistance and market development for critical infrastructure facilities (e.g., hospitals, military bases, wastewater treatment facilities) and to support other applications.

The House bill recommends a $5 million increase over the FY2013 estimate, while the Senate bill proposes an increase of $101 million (87%) over FY2013.

Federal Energy Management Program (FEMP)

FEMP provides expertise, training, and other services to help federal agencies achieve congressionally mandated energy efficiency and renewable energy goals. DOE requests $36 million, which would be about $6 million more than the FY2012 DOE estimate. (The House bill

---

[34] Going forward, DOE expects to establish CEMIs as an alternative to the concept of "manufacturing demonstration facilities" (MDFs), which it implemented in FY2012 with the establishment of the Critical Materials Hub (discussed in the next paragraph). DOE's Oak Ridge National Laboratory is the home for AMO's first MDF focused on additive manufacturing and low-cost carbon fiber. For more on MDFs, see http://www1.eere.energy.gov/manufacturing/rd/m/mdf.html.

[35] The Hub also supports materials needs for defense and other strategic industries.

did not provide an FY2013 estimate.) A new subprogram, the Federal Energy Efficiency Fund, would get $10 million to provide leverage for cost sharing of capital improvement projects at federal agencies. The House bill recommends zero funding—termination of the program. The Senate bill proposes maintaining funding at the FY2013 level.

Program Direction

This administrative program funds federal employees, contract support, and operational costs. DOE requests $185 million, about a $20 million increase over the FY2013 DOE-estimated level (the House bill combined EERE with EDER management—there is no separate FY2013 estimate for EERE.) The increase would cover an EERE reorganization that would consolidate information technology and establish an active project management (APM) system to oversee competitive grants and cooperative agreements.

Strategic Programs

For this program (formerly Program Support), DOE seeks $36 million, an increase of $11 million over the FY2013 estimate. Of that amount, $7 million would go to a new effort to increase the rate of clean energy technology commercialization from the national labs. The other $4 million of the increase would expand efforts to evaluate EERE's impacts and returns on investment. The House bill recommends a $23 million (92%) cut from the FY2013 estimate, while the Senate bill proposes an increase of $3 million (12%) over FY2013.

Weatherization Grant Program

This program addresses regulatory, financial, and planning barriers faced by state and local governments. The goal is to foster technologies, practices, and policies that support state and local governments in providing home energy services to low-income families that help them reduce energy costs and save money. DOE requests $184 million, a $116 million increase over the FY2013 estimate. DOE says that many states have expended leftover Recovery Act funds and now need new funds to avoid cutting core programs and services.[36] The House bill recommends a $10 million (14%) increase over the FY2013 estimate, while the Senate bill proposes an increase of $116 million (172%) over FY2013.

State Energy Grant Program

This program supports both administrative and program activities at many state energy offices. DOE requests $57 million, a $7 million increase over the FY2013 estimate. The increase would support competitive projects that address barriers to an effort that aims to cut state energy use by 1% annually. The House bill recommends a $38 million (76%) cut from the FY2013 estimate, while the Senate bill proposes a small increase of $3 million (7%) over FY2013.

---

[36] Also, in FY2014, collection and analysis of data from ARRA projects would enable updated estimates of program energy savings, cost savings, leveraged funds, and other impacts. For more details about the program see CRS Report R42147, *DOE Weatherization Program: A Review of Funding, Performance, and Cost-Effectiveness Studies*, by Fred Sissine.

Electricity Delivery and Energy Reliability (EDER) Program[37]

DOE requests $169 million—a net increase of $32 million over the FY2013 DOE estimate—which includes $20 million for a new Electricity Systems Hub. The Hub would address the growing need for the grid to accommodate renewables, the impact of electric vehicles and distributed generation, and the advent of smart grid equipment. The Hub funding would be mostly offset by cuts to other programs. Also, notable increases are sought for three subprograms: infrastructure security ($10 million), cybersecurity ($9 million), and clean energy transmission ($7 million). Offsetting reductions would come from two subprograms: smart grid (-$9 million) and energy storage (-$4 million). The House bill recommends merging EERE and EDER and does not provide a separate breakout for the entire EDER program. The Senate bill proposes $20 million less than the request.

Nuclear Energy[38]

The Obama Administration's FY2014 funding request for nuclear energy research and development totals $735.5 million. Including advanced reactors, fuel cycle technology, infrastructure support, and safeguards and security, the total nuclear energy request is $22.0 million (3%) below the FY2013 funding level. Funding for safeguards and security at DOE's Idaho facilities in FY2013 was provided under a separate appropriations account, Other Defense Activities, but it is included under the Nuclear Energy account in the FY2014 request. In contrast, funding for space and defense infrastructure, totaling $64.1 million in the FY2013 nuclear energy appropriation, would be shifted to the National Aeronautics and Space Administration (NASA) by the Administration's request. The largest proposed reductions for FY2014 are Reactor Concepts (-34.5%), Nuclear Energy Enabling Technologies (-12.6%), and Fuel Cycle R&D (-8.8%). A 4.5% increase is requested for Small Modular Reactor Licensing Technical Support.

The House-passed bill would provide $656.4 million for nuclear energy. That total excludes the Administration's proposed shift of $94.0 million for Idaho safeguards and security from Other Defense Activities and includes the space and defense funding transfer to NASA. For the programs that would remain in nuclear energy, therefore, the House bill would provide an increase of $14.9 million from the Administration request and a decrease of $37 million from FY2013. The Senate Appropriations Committee recommended the same total as the Administration request, including the proposed funding transfers.

The Administration's FY2014 nuclear R&D budget request is consistent with DOE's *Nuclear Energy Research and Development Roadmap* issued in April 2010.[39] The Roadmap lays out the following four main goals for the program:

- Develop technologies and other solutions that can improve the reliability, sustain the safety, and extend the life of current reactors;

---

[37] This section was prepared by Fred Sissine.

[38] This section was prepared by Mark Holt.

[39] Department of Energy, *Nuclear Energy Research and Development Roadmap*, Report to Congress, Washington, DC, April 2010, http://nuclear.gov/pdfFiles/NuclearEnergy_Roadmap_Final.pdf.

- Develop improvements in the affordability of new reactors to enable nuclear energy to help meet the Administration's energy security and climate change goals;

- Develop sustainable nuclear fuel cycles; and

- Understand and minimize the risks of nuclear proliferation and terrorism.

The Senate Appropriations Committee directed DOE to update the *Roadmap* within 180 days after enactment to reflect lessons learned from the Fukushima nuclear accident, advances in small modular reactors, and the Administration's new nuclear waste strategy.

Reactor Concepts

The Reactor Concepts program area includes the Next Generation Nuclear Plant (NGNP) demonstration project and research on other advanced reactors (often referred to as Generation IV reactors). This area also includes funding for developing advanced small modular reactors (discussed in the next section) and to enhance the "sustainability" of existing commercial light water reactors. The total FY2014 funding request for this program is $72.5 million, a reduction of $41.6 million from FY2013. The House voted to provide $86.5 million, while the Senate Appropriations Committee approved the Administration's funding level.

Most of the Administration's proposed reduction in Reactor Concepts would be for NGNP, a high-temperature gas-cooled reactor demonstration project authorized by the Energy Policy Act of 2005 (EPACT05, P.L. 109-58). The reactor is intended to produce high-temperature heat that could be used to generate electricity, help separate hydrogen from water, or be used in other industrial processes. DOE is not requesting any funding specifically for the NGNP project in FY2014. Under EPACT05, the Secretary of Energy was to decide by the end of FY2011 whether to proceed toward construction of a demonstration plant. Secretary of Energy Steven Chu informed Congress on October 17, 2011, that DOE would not proceed with a demonstration plant design "at this time" but would continue research on the technology.[40] Potential obstacles facing NGNP include low prices for natural gas, the major competing fuel, and private-sector unwillingness to share the project's costs as required by EPACT05.[41] According to the DOE budget justification, some research activities now conducted under the NGNP program will be shifted to the Advanced Reactor Concepts subprogram in FY2014.

Funding for the Advanced Reactor Concepts subprogram would be increased by the Administration request to $31.0 million in FY2014, up from $21.7 million in FY2012. The increase would cover research on high-temperature gas reactors previously conducted under the NGNP Program. Reactor concepts being developed by the Advanced Reactor Concepts subprogram are generally classified as "Generation IV" reactors, as opposed to the existing fleet of commercial light water reactors, which are generally classified as generations II and III. Such advanced reactors "could dramatically improve nuclear power performance including sustainability, economics, and safety and proliferation resistance," according to the FY2014 justification. Nuclear technology development under this program includes "fast reactors," using high-energy neutrons, and reactors that would use a variety of heat-transfer fluids, such as liquid

---

[40] Idaho National Laboratory, *NGNP Project 2011 Status and Path Forward*, INL/EXT-11-23907, December 2011.

[41] Yanmei Xie, "Cheap Natural Gas, Cost-Share Disagreement Jeopardize NGNP," *Nucleonics Week*, April 28, 2011, p. 1.

sodium and supercritical carbon dioxide. International research collaboration in this area would continue under the Generation IV International Forum (GIF). The House bill would boost Advanced Reactor Concepts funding to $45 million, with the increase focused on high-temperature gas reactor fuel development formerly conducted under the NGNP program.

DOE's FY2014 request for the Light Water Reactor Sustainability subprogram is $21.5 million, $3.3 million below the FY2012 appropriation. The program conducts research on extending the life of existing commercial light water reactors beyond 60 years, the maximum operating period currently licensed by the Nuclear Regulatory Commission. The program, which is to be cost-shared with the nuclear industry, is to study the aging of reactor materials and analyze safety margins of aging plants. Other research under this program is to focus on improving the efficiency of existing plants, through such measures as increasing plant capacity and upgrading instrumentation and control systems. Research on longer-life LWR fuel is aimed at eliminating radioactive leakage from nuclear fuel and increasing its accident tolerance, along with other "post-Fukushima lessons learned," according to the budget justification. The House approved the Administration funding level, as did the Senate committee.

Small Modular Reactors

Rising cost estimates for large conventional nuclear reactors—widely projected to be $6 billion or more—have contributed to growing interest in proposals for small modular reactors (SMRs). Ranging from about 40 to 300 megawatts of electrical capacity, such reactors would be only a fraction of the size of current commercial reactors. Several modular reactors would be installed together to make up a power block with a single control room, under most concepts. Current SMR proposals would use a variety of technologies, including the high-temperature gas technology described above and the light water (LWR) technology used by today's commercial reactors.

DOE requested $70.0 million for FY2014 to provide technical support for licensing small modular reactors, about $3 million above the FY2013 funding level. This program has focused on LWR designs because they are believed most likely to be deployed in the near term, according to DOE. The FY2014 budget justification states that the SMR licensing and technical support program will last six years and cost DOE a total of $452 million. The program is similar to DOE's support for larger commercial reactor designs under the Nuclear Power 2010 Program, which ended in FY2010. DOE will provide support for design certification, standards, and licensing. As with the Nuclear Power 2010 Program, at least half the costs of the SMR design and licensing program are to be covered by industry partners, according to DOE.

A consortium led by Babcock & Wilcox (B&W) was announced by DOE in November 2012 as the first award recipient under the program.[42] DOE and the B&W consortium signed a cooperative agreement in April 2013 to implement the award, allowing for federal payments of around $226 million over five years to design and license a commercial demonstration plant that could open by 2022.[43] DOE announced a second award solicitation in March 2013 for innovative SMR designs that could begin commercial operation around 2025.[44]

---

[42] DOE, "Energy Department Announces New Investment in U.S. Small Modular Reactor Design and Commercialization," news release, November 20, 2012, http://energy.gov/articles/energy-department-announces-new-investment-us-small-modular-reactor-design-and.

[43] B&W, "B&W, DOE Sign Cooperative Agreement for Small Modular Reactor Funding," news release, April 15, (continued...)

The House bill would increase funding for SMR design and licensing support to $110.0 million, while the Senate Appropriations Committee recommended the Administration level.

An additional $20.0 million for FY2014 was requested by DOE under the Reactor Concepts program (described in the section above) for SMR advanced concepts R&D—$4.5 million below the FY2012 funding level. Unlike the SMR licensing support program, which focuses on near-term technology, the SMR advanced concepts program would conduct research on technologies that might be deployed in the longer term, according to the budget justification. The House approved the Administration funding level, as did the Senate panel.

Small modular reactors would go against the overall trend in nuclear power technology toward ever-larger reactors intended to spread construction costs over a greater output of electricity. Proponents of small reactors contend that they would be economically viable despite their far lower electrical output because modules could be assembled in factories and shipped to plant sites, with minimal on-site fabrication, and because their smaller size would allow for simpler safety systems. In addition, although modular plants might have similar or higher costs per kilowatt-hour than conventional large reactors, their ability to be constructed in smaller increments could reduce electric utilities' financial commitment and risk.

Fuel Cycle Research and Development

The Fuel Cycle Research and Development Program conducts "long-term, science-based" research on a wide variety of technologies for improving the management of spent nuclear fuel, according to the DOE budget justification. The total FY2014 funding request for this program is $165.1 million, $10.1 million below the FY2013 appropriation. The House bill would provide $91.1 million, while the Senate Appropriations Committee recommended $175.1 million.

The range of fuel cycle technologies being studied by the program includes direct disposal of spent fuel (the "once through" cycle) and partial and full recycling, according to the FY2014 budget justification. The Fuel Cycle R&D Program "will research and develop a suite of technology options that will enable future decision-makers to make informed decisions about how best to manage nuclear waste and used fuel from reactors," the budget justification says.

Much of the Administration's planned research on spent fuel management options would address the near-term recommendations of the Blue Ribbon Commission on America's Nuclear Future, which issued its final report on January 26, 2012.[45] The commission was chartered to develop alternatives to the planned Yucca Mountain, NV, spent fuel repository, which President Obama wants to terminate. DOE released its *Strategy for the Management and Disposal of Used Nuclear Fuel and High-Level Radioactive Waste* in January 2013 in response to the Blue Ribbon Commission report. Funding to begin implementing the strategy is included in the Used Nuclear

---

(...continued)

2013, http://www.babcock.com/news_and_events/2013/20130415a.html.

[44] DOE, "Energy Department Announces New Funding Opportunity for Innovative Small Modular Reactors," news release, March 11, 2013, http://energy.gov/articles/energy-department-announces-new-funding-opportunity-innovative-small-modular-reactors.

[45] Blue Ribbon Commission on America's Nuclear Future, "Blue Ribbon Commission on America's Nuclear Future Issues Final Report to Secretary of Energy," press release, January 26, 2012, http://brc.gov/index.php?q=announcement/brc-releases-their-final-report.

Fuel Disposition subprogram, with a request of $60.0 million, $2.1 million above the FY2012 funding level. Activities in that area include developing plans for a "consent-based siting process" for nuclear storage and disposal facilities, waste transportation analyses, and research on potential waste repositories, including salt caverns and deep boreholes. (See the "Nuclear Waste Disposal" section, below, for more details.)

Other major research areas in the Fuel Cycle R&D Program include the development of accident-tolerant fuels for existing commercial reactors, evaluation of fuel cycle options, development of improved technologies to prevent diversion of nuclear materials for weapons, and technology to increase nuclear fuel resources, such as uranium extraction from seawater. The Senate Appropriations Committee increased the Administration's request for the Advanced Fuels subprogram by $20 million, to $57.1 million, with an emphasis on developing "meltdown-resistant nuclear fuels" that could be tested and made available within 10 years.

Nuclear Energy Enabling Technologies

The Nuclear Energy Enabling Technologies (NEET) program "is designed to conduct research and development (R&D) in crosscutting technologies that directly support and enable the development of new and advanced reactor designs and fuel cycle technologies," according to the FY2014 DOE budget justification. The DOE funding request for the program is $62.3 million, $11.6 million below the FY2013 level. The House bill includes $66.7 million for the program, while the Senate Appropriations Committee approved the level sought by the Administration.

DOE's proposed funding cuts would come from the categories of Crosscutting Technology Development, for which $13.9 million was requested, $5.9 million below FY2012, and Nuclear Energy Advanced Modeling and Simulation, which would be reduced from $13.9 million to $9.5 million. According to the budget justification, the cuts result from reducing research on manufacturing methods and shifting proliferation and terrorism risk assessments to the Fuel Cycle R&D Program. Continuing crosscutting research activities are to include development of innovative materials, harsh environment sensors, and fully digital reactor control systems.

The Energy Innovation Hub for Modeling and Simulation (separate from the Nuclear Energy Advanced Modeling and Simulation subprogram), has a request of $24.3 million, slightly below the FY2012 appropriation. The Modeling and Simulation Hub is creating a computer model of an operating reactor to allow a better understanding of nuclear technology, with the benefits of such modeling extending to other energy technologies in the future, according to the budget justification.

DOE requested $14.6 million for the National Scientific User Facility, $500,000 above the FY2012 appropriation, to support partnerships by universities and other research organizations to conduct experiments "at facilities not normally accessible to these organizations," according to the justification. In addition to previously awarded projects, one new long-term project is expected to be fully funded in FY2014, under the budget request.

Fossil Energy Research and Development[46]

For FY2014, the Obama Administration requested $420.575 million for the Fossil Energy Research and Development Program with the provision that it remain available until expended and that $115.753 million remain available until September 30, 2015 for program direction. The request represents a 21% decrease from the FY2013 Appropriation (**Table 10**).

The Obama Administration proposed a new budget structure for the FY2012 Fossil Energy Research and Development (FER&D) program that emphasized coal with a focus on carbon capture and storage (CCS) technologies. The FY2012 appropriations bill adopted the new structure. The CCS program intends to demonstrate advanced clean coal technologies on a commercial-project scale, and build and operate near-zero atmospheric emissions power plants that capture and store carbon dioxide (CO2). A Carbon Capture sub-program focuses on separating CO2 in both pre-combustion and post-combustion systems. The Carbon Storage sub-program focuses on long-term geologic storage of CO2, including small- and large-scale CO2 injection tests. An Advanced Energy Systems sub-program focuses on improving the efficiency of coal-based power systems to capture CO2. The Advanced Energy Systems sub-program focuses on improving the efficiency of coal-based power systems, enabling affordable CO2 capture, increasing plant availability, and maintaining the highest environmental standards. The Cross-Cutting Research activity serves as a bridge between basic and applied research by fostering the development and deployment of innovative systems.

For FY2014, the House bill would appropriate $450.0 million for Fossil Energy Research and Development, $29.4 million above the President's budget request. The bill directs DOE to use $8.7 million in prior-year balances, as proposed in the budget request. The bill breaks out:

- $315.9 million for Coal with $68.9 million applied to Carbon Capture (under which no funding shall be applied to a Natural Gas Capture Prize) and $79.3 million applied to Carbon Storage (to include $7.5 million for additional support of Enhanced Oil Recovery).

- $91.7 million for Advanced Energy Systems, with $25.0 million applied to solid oxide fuel cell systems, $5.0 million to coal-biomass to liquids activities, $5.0 million to High Performance Materials within Advanced Combustion Systems, and $8.0 million to Gasification Systems.

- $30.9 million for Cross Cutting Research, with $5.0 million applied to Advanced Ultra Super Critical Program.

- $45.0 million for NETL Coal Research and Development with $10 million applied to research in recovering rare earth elements from coal.

- $115.8 million for Program Direction.

- $7.2 million for Natural Gas Technologies, with no new funding applied to the proposed joint research effort with the Environmental Protection Agency and the Department of the Interior into hydraulic fracturing technologies, $5.0 million for research into the cost-effective and responsible extraction of methane hydrates, and $2.2 million for continuing the Risk Based Data Management System.

---

[46] This section was prepared by Anthony Andrews.

For FY2014, the Senate committee recommends $420.6 million for Fossil Energy Research and Development, the same as the President's request. The committee recommendation breaks out:

- $268.6 million for CCS and Power Systems, with $40.0 million applied to Advanced Energy Systems and $8.0 million to continue Gasification Systems activities.

- $115.8 million for Program Direction.

- $13.3 million for Plant and Capital Equipment.

- $5.9 million for Fossil Energy Environmental Restoration.

- $0.7 million for Special Recruitment Programs.

- Within available funds, the committee directs the department to continue the Risk Based Data Management System.

The committee recommended $20 million for Natural Gas Technologies, including $12.0 million for interagency research and development initiatives and $8.0 million for ongoing methane hydrates research and development.

Table 10. Fossil Energy Research and Development

($ millions)

	FY2013 Approp.[a]	FY2014 Request	House	Senate	Conf.
Coal					
Carbon Capture	68.9	112.0	68.9	112.0	
Carbon Storage	115.5	61.1	79.3	61.1	
Advanced Energy Systems	100.0	48.0	91.7	40.0	
Cross Cutting Research	49.2	20.5	30.9	20.5	
National Energy Tech. Lab Coal R&D	35.0	35.0	45.0	35.0	
Coal Subtotal	**368.6**	**276.6**	315.8	268.6	
Natural Gas Technologies	15.0	17.0	7.2	20.0	
Unconventional Fossil Energy				5.0	
Program Direction	120.0	115.8	115.8	115.7	
Plant and Capital Equipment	16.8	13.3	13.3	13.3	
F E Environmental Restoration	7.9	5.9	5.9	5.9	
Special Recruitment Program	0.7	0.7	0.7	0.7	
Subtotal	**534.0**	**420.3**	**458.7**	**429.3**	
Use of Prior Year Balance		**-8.7**	**-8.7**	**-8.7**	

	FY2013 Approp.[a]	FY2014 Request	House	Senate	Conf.
Total	534.0	420.6	450.0	420.6	

Source: FY2014 Budget Request; H.Rept. 113-135; S.Rept. 113-47.

Notes: Coal was formerly Carbon Capture and Sequestration Demonstration.

a. Source: H.Rept. 113-135. Figures do not reflect the March 1, 2013, sequester of funds under P.L. 112-25.

Strategic Petroleum Reserve[47]

The Strategic Petroleum Reserve (SPR), authorized by the Energy Policy and Conservation Act (P.L. 94-163) in 1975, consists of caverns formed out of naturally occurring salt domes in Louisiana and Texas. The SPR provides strategic and economic security against foreign and domestic disruptions in U.S. oil supplies via an emergency stockpile of crude oil. The program fulfills U.S. obligations under the International Energy Program, which avails the United States of International Energy Agency (IEA) assistance through its coordinated energy emergency response plans, and provides a deterrent against energy supply disruptions.

By early 2010, the SPR's maximum capacity reached 727 million barrels.[48] The federal government has not purchased oil for the SPR since 1994. Beginning in 2000, additions to the SPR were made with royalty-in-kind (RIK) oil acquired by the Department of Energy in lieu of cash royalties paid on production from federal offshore leases. In September 2009 the Secretary of the Interior announced a transitional phasing out of the RIK Program.[49]

In its FY2012 request, the Obama Administration proposed a sale of $500 million in petroleum from the SPR, to be completed not later than March 1, 2012, for deposit in the General Fund of the Treasury. In summer 2011, the President ordered an SPR sale in coordination with an International Energy Administration sale under treaty obligation. The U.S. sale of 30.6 million barrels reduced the SPR inventory to 695.9 million barrels.

For FY2014, the Administration requested $189.4 million to operate the SPR, a decrease from the $192.7 million enacted in for FY2012.

The House Committee recommended $189.4 million for operating the Strategic Petroleum Reserve, the same as the budget request.

The Senate Committee recommended $189.4 million for the operating the Strategic Petroleum Reserve.

---

[47] This section was prepared by Anthony Andrews.

[48] For details on the SPR see CRS Report R41687, *The Strategic Petroleum Reserve and Refined Product Reserves: Authorization and Drawdown Policy*, by Anthony Andrews and Robert Pirog.

[49] Bureau of Ocean Management, Regulation and Enforcement. http://www.mrm.boemre.gov/AssetManagement/ default.htm.

Science[50]

The DOE Office of Science conducts basic research in six program areas: advanced scientific computing research, basic energy sciences, biological and environmental research, fusion energy sciences, high-energy physics, and nuclear physics. Through these programs, DOE is the third-largest federal funder of basic research and the largest federal funder of research in the physical sciences.[51] **Table 11** includes the FY2012 current plan, FY2014 request, and House and Senate appropriations committee recommendations for Office of Science accounts.

For FY2014, DOE requests $5.153 billion for the Office of Science, an increase of 5.9% ($287 million) from the FY2013 pre-sequestration, post-rescission amount of $4.866 billion. As passed by the House, H.R. 2609 (Energy and Water Development and Related Agencies Appropriations Act, 2014) would provide $4.653 billion to the Office of Science in FY2014. This amount is $500 million (9.7%) less than the Administration's request. The amount recommended by the Senate Committee on Appropriations ($5.153 billion) is the same as the request.[52] H.Rept. 113-135, which accompanied H.R. 2609 when it was reported from the House Committee on Appropriations, raises general concerns about the percentage of Office of Science funding committed to ongoing projects each year.[53] The House report[54] and bill include language designed to limit this practice.

Table 11. Science

($ millions)

Program	FY2013 Approp.[a]	FY2014 Request	House	Senate	Conf.
Advanced Scientific Computing Research	440.9	465.6	432.4	493.8	
Basic Energy Sciences	1,689.5	1,862.4	1,583.1	1,805.2	
Biological and Environmental Research	610.2	625.3	494.1	625.3	
Fusion Energy Sciences	401.1	458.3	506.1	458.3	
High Energy Physics	789.6	776.5	772.5	806.6	
Nuclear Physics	548.5	569.9	551.9	569.9	
Workforce Development for Teachers and Scientists	18.5	16.5	16.5	16.5	
Science Laboratories Infrastructure	111.5	97.8	46.6	97.8	

---

[50] This section was prepared by Heather Gonzalez.

[51] Based on preliminary FY2012 data from Tables 29 and 22 of National Science Foundation, National Center for Science and Engineering Statistics, *Federal Funds for Research and Development: Fiscal Years 2009-11*, NSF 13-326 (July 2013).

[52] S. 1245 (Energy and Water Development and Related Agencies Appropriations Act, 2014) and S.Rept. 113-47, which accompanied S. 1245 when it was reported from the Senate Committee on Appropriations. This section refers to S.Rept. 113-47 as the "Senate report."

[53] On page 10, H.Rept. 113-135, the House Committee on Appropriations states, "Most of its [Office of Science] new multi-year awards continue to be mortgaged against out-year funding. Most of the new awards are small and should be fully funded. In fiscal year 2013, more than 70 percent of Science's multi-year awards were valued at less than $1,500,000. In a nearly $5,000,000,000 account, this practice of carrying mortgages for smaller awards is avoidable and should be terminated." The House Committee on Appropriations raised similar concerns about various Department of Energy accounts in FY2013 (see H.Rept. 112-462) and FY2012 (see H.Rept. 112-118).

[54] This section refers to H.Rept. 113-135 as the "House report."

Program	FY2013 Approp.[a]	FY2014 Request	House	Senate	Conf.
Safeguards and Security	81.8	87.0	85.0	87.0	
Science Program Direction	184.6	193.3	174.9	192.3	
Use of Prior Year Funds	0.0	0.0	-10.0	0.0	
Total	**4,876.0**	**5,152.8**	**4,653.0**	**5,152.8**	

Source: FY2014 DOE budget request; H.Rept. 113-135; S.Rept. 113-47.

a.   Source: H.Rept. 113-135. Figures do not reflect the March 1, 2013, sequester of funds under P.L. 112-25.

Since FY2006, overall increases in the Office of Science budget have been at least partially driven by the so-called "doubling path" policy. Under this policy, Congress and successive Administrations sought to double the combined funding for the Office of Science, the National Science Foundation, and the National Institute of Standards and Technology's core laboratory and construction accounts (collectively "the targeted accounts").[55] However, actual funding for the targeted accounts has not typically reached annual authorized levels. The current authorization ends in FY2013. It is unclear whether policymakers will continue the doubling path policy in FY2014. In FY2013 some legislators raised concerns about the doubling effort given the nation's fiscal challenges.[56] On the other hand, some analysts believe that without the doubling path policy in place, funding levels for targeted accounts might have fallen over the past half-decade.[57]

The FY2014 request for the largest Office of Science program, Basic Energy Sciences (BES), is $1.862 billion. This amount is $218 million (13.2%) more than the FY2012 funding level of $1.645 million. Most of the BES increase would fund scientific user facilities (59%) and Energy Frontier Research Centers (EFRC)/Energy Innovation Hubs (32%). The FY2014 BES request for scientific user facilities includes, among other things, increased operations funding for synchrotron radiation light sources, high-flux neutron sources, and Nanoscale Science Research Centers. As planned, construction funding for the LINAC Coherent Light Source-II (LCLS-II) would increase by $65 million,[58] and funding for the National Synchrotron Light Source-II (NSLS-II) would decrease by $125 million compared to FY2012 funding levels. DOE indicates that it will issue a solicitation for new and existing EFRCs in FY2014.

The House would provide $1.583 billion for BES in FY2014. This amount is $279 million (15.0%) less than the Administration's FY2014 request. The Senate report recommends $1.805 billion for this account in FY2014. Both appropriations committees recommend the requested level ($24 million each) for the *Fuels from Sunlight* and *Battery and Energy Storage* Energy Innovation Hubs. The committees differ on funding for the Experimental Program to Stimulate Competitive Research (EPSCoR)—which the Senate committee would fund ($20 million) and the House committee would not—and on funding for EFRCs. The Senate report recommends $100

---

[55] For further analysis of the doubling effort, see CRS Report R41951, *An Analysis of Efforts to Double Federal Funding for Physical Sciences and Engineering Research*, by John F. Sargent Jr.

[56] For example, see Opening Statement of Ranking Member Dan Lipinski, in U.S. Congress, House Committee on Science, Space, and Technology, Subcommittee on Research and Science Education, "The National Science Foundation's FY2013 Budget Request," hearings, 112th Cong., 2nd sess., February 28, 2012.

[57] For example, see testimony of Dr. Jeffrey L. Furman, in U.S. Congress, Senate Committee on Commerce, Science, and Transportation, "Five Years of the America COMPETES Act: Progress, Challenges, and Next Steps," hearings, 112th Cong., 2nd sess., September 19, 2012.

[58] DOE's FY2012 budget included $30 million in Major Items of Equipment funding for the LCLS-II.

million for EFRCs in FY2014. The House would provide $60 million. Neither committee appears to provide requested one-time funds for EFRCs.[59] The House report cautions the department against assuming BES budget growth in future years and provides funding for certain BES activities, including the NSLS-II Experimental Tools ($25 million) as well as an unspecified amount for the first year of funding for the LCLS-II two-tunnel upgrade.

In percentage terms, the largest increase in the FY2014 Office of Science budget request is for the Fusion Energy Sciences (FES) program. The FY2014 FES request for $485 million is $65 million (17%) more than the FY2012 level. Funding for facilities would increase by $102 million while funding for the science category would decrease by $32 million. The requested increase for FES facilities is driven by the request for the U.S. contribution to the International Thermonuclear Experimental Reactor (ITER). ITER is a fusion research facility currently under construction in France. The FY2014 request for the U.S. contribution to ITER is $225 million, an increase of $120 million over the FY2012 level.[60] Funding for domestic fusion activities would decrease; including funding for the Alcator C-Mod tokamak, a fusion reactor that the Administration planned to shut down in FY2013. Policymakers and fusion researchers have long been concerned about the impact of ITER's funding needs on the availability of resources for the domestic fusion program.

The House would provide $506 million for FES in FY2014. This amount is $48 million (10.4%) more than both the Administration's request. The Senate report recommends $458 million, which is the same as the request. The House would include $22 million for the Alcator C-Mod; the Senate report specifically excludes funding for this project. The Senate report recommends $75 million for the Princeton Plasma Physics Laboratory, $77 million for the DIII-D fusion reactor, $15 million for High Energy Density Laboratory Plasmas, and $12 million for the Fusion Simulation program. With respect to ITER, both the House and Senate appropriations committee reports include language seeking an updated project baseline and cost schedule for ITER. The Senate report further states that funds shall not be available for the U.S. contribution to ITER until the DOE submits these materials. The House would provide $218 million for ITER in FY2014; the Senate Committee on Appropriations recommends $184 million. Both appropriations committees direct DOE to submit a 10-year plan for the FES program.

For High Energy Physics (HEP), the request is $777 million, an increase of $6 million from FY2012. The FY2014 HEP budget request has been restructured from prior years.[61] According to the request, in FY2014 HEP seeks to shift funding from research categories to support full operations of existing facilities and experiments, the planned construction funding profile of the

---

[59] H.Rept. 113-135 specifically states that the recommendation does not include $68.7 million in one-time funding. S.Rept. 113-47 does not specifically exclude one-time funding, but the amount provided ($100.0 million) is $68.7 million less than the total FY2014 request for $168.7 million, which includes $68.7 million in one-time funding.

[60] In 2008, the cost for the U.S. share of ITER was estimated to be between $1.45 billion and $2.2 billion. Schedule delays, design and scope changes, and other factors have placed upward pressure of ITER costs and delayed formal approval of a revised cost estimate. Pending a new official estimate, DOE asserts that funding of $225 million per year will allow it to meet international obligations—up to the achievement of ITR's "first plasma" milestone—for a total cost of $2.4 billion.

[61] For more information about these changes, see U.S. Department of Energy, Office of Chief Financial Officer, *FY2014 Congressional Budget Request,* vol. 4, April 2013, p. SC-210. The Office of Science FY2014 budget request states that the HEP budget restructuring is consistent with the long-range plan published in U.S. Department of Energy, Office of Science, and National Science Foundation, Particle Physics Prioritization Panel, *U.S. Particle Physics: Scientific Opportunities for the Next Ten Years,* May 29, 2008, http://science.energy.gov/~/media/hep/pdf/files/pdfs/ p5_report_06022008.pdf.

Muon to Electron Conversion Experiment (Mu2e), and fabrication of an experiment to measure the muon anomalous magnetic moment. Funding is also requested to support the Large Synoptic Survey Telescope camera—a joint activity with the National Science Foundation—and U.S. contributions to the upgrade of the Belle detector in Japan.

The House would provide $773 million for HEP in FY2014. This amount is $4 million less than the Administration's request. The Senate Committee on Appropriations, on the other hand, recommends increasing HEP funding by $30 million over the requested level (to $807 million). Both committees recommend $35 million for Mu2e. The House would include $8 million for Long Baseline Neutrino Experiment (LBNE) project engineering and design, but would exclude funding for long-lead procurement and construction. The Senate report recommends $20 million for LBNE project engineering and design as well as $10 million for research and development.

The request for Biological and Environmental Research (BER) is $625 million, an increase of $33 million from FY2012. About two-thirds of the increase would go to Foundational Genomics Research (40%), Terrestrial Ecosystem Science (15%), and the Atmospheric Radiation Measurement Climate Research Facility (10%). The FY2014 budget request reduces funding in Radiological Sciences and establishes a new Mesoscale to Molecules program. Other Biological Systems Science programs are generally near FY2012 levels. The Administration seeks a 7% reduction from the FY2012 level for the Environmental Molecular Science Laboratory funding. Most other Climate and Environmental Sciences programs are near FY2012 levels.

The House would reduce BER funding (compared to the FY2014 request) by $131 million (21%) in FY2014. The Senate Committee on Appropriations recommends $625 million, which is the requested level. The House report expresses support for biomass research and recommends the requested level ($75 million) for BioEnergy Research Centers. Among other things, the Senate report recommends the requested levels of $321 million and $304 million, respectively, for Biological Systems Science and Climate and Environmental Sciences.

For Nuclear Physics (NP), the request is $570 million, up $35 million from FY2012. Medium Energy Nuclear Physics (MENP) operations and the Facility for Rare Isotope Beams at Michigan State University (FRIB) would receive most of the proposed increase. The FY2014 budget request for MENP includes funding for, among other things, initiation of beam development and commissioning activities at the Continuous Electron Beam Accelerator Facility (CEBAF). The FY2104 request indicates that these increases in CEBAF operations funding are at least partially offset by planned construction funding decreases for the 12GeV CEBAF Upgrade. Funding increases for the FRIB would support the continuation of planned construction activities and major procurements.

The House would provide $552 million (3.2% below the requested level) for NP in FY2014. The Senate Committee on Appropriations recommends the requested level of $570 million. Both committee reports recommend $55 million for FRIB construction, $26 million in construction funds for the 12 GeV CEBAF Upgrade, and $165 million to support approximately 22 weeks of operations for the Relativistic Heavy Ion Collider (RHIC). (These amounts are equal to requested levels for these activities.) Additionally, the Senate report recommends $17 million for the Argonne Tandem Linac Accelerator System.

The request for Advanced Scientific Computing Research (ASCR) is $466 million, an increase of $37 million over the FY2012 level. The FY2014 request seeks increases in funding for most

ASCR programs. Two ASCR programs—Leadership Computing Facilities and High Performance Network Facilities and Testbeds (ESNet)—would receive decreases.

The House would provide $432 million—$33 million or 7.1% below the request—to ASCR in FY2014. The Senate Committee on Appropriations recommends $494 million—$28 million or 6.0% more than the request. Almost half of the increase over requested levels ($12.5 million) in the Senate report is driven by increased funding for exascale computing. The Senate report recommends a total of $150 million, $81 million of which would come from the ACSR account, for exascale computing in FY2014. The House would provide $69 million in ACSR funding for exascale computing (the requested level) in FY2014. For Leadership Computing Facilities the House would provide $149 million (slightly more than the request) while the Senate report recommends $160 million, or $13 million more than the request. The Senate report recommends $66 million, equal to the request, for High Performance Production Computing. The House would provide $62 million. The House would also provide the requested level ($33 million) for ESNet. The Senate report recommends $6 million for the Computational Science Graduate Fellowship (CSGF), which the Administration had proposed terminating and funding through the National Science Foundation instead.[62] The House implicitly accepts the termination of the CSGF program.[63]

ARPA-E[64]

The Advanced Research Projects Agency–Energy (ARPA-E) was authorized by the America COMPETES Act (P.L. 110-69) to support transformational energy technology research projects. It received its first funding in FY2009, mostly through the American Recovery and Reinvestment Act of 2009 (P.L. 111-5), and announced its first round of contract awards in October 2009. DOE budget documents describe ARPA-E's mission as overcoming long-term, high-risk technological barriers to the development of energy technologies. The FY2014 request for ARPA-E is $379 million, an increase of $104 million from FY2012. As in FY2013, the FY2014 ARPA-E request includes two research thrust areas: Transportation Systems ($197 million requested) and Stationary Power Systems ($148 million requested).

As amended on the floor of the House, H.R. 2609 (Energy and Water Development and Related Agencies Appropriations Act, 2014) would provide $70 million for ARPA-E in FY2014. As reported by the Senate Appropriations committee, S. 1245 (Energy and Water Development and Related Agencies Appropriations Act, 2014) would provide $379 million for ARPA-E. S.Rept. 113-47 directs ARPA-E to evaluate the success of the first set of projects and report to the Appropriations Committee on the findings of the evaluation.

---

[62] The Obama Administration seeks to reorganize and consolidate federal science, technology, engineering, and mathematics (STEM) education programs in FY2014. As part of this effort, the Administration proposed the transfer and consolidation of certain federal fellowships (including the CSGF) within the National Science Foundation's Graduate Research Fellowship program (GRF).

[63] H.Rept. 113-135 contains general provisions that prohibit the department from funding fellowships and scholarships unless those programs are specifically provided for in either the department's budget justification or H.Rept. 113-135. Neither document provided funding for the CSGF in FY2014.

[64] This section was prepared by Heather Gonzalez. Previous versions of this section were prepared by Daniel Morgan.

Nuclear Waste Disposal[65]

The Administration's FY2014 budget includes no funding for DOE's Office of Civilian Radioactive Waste Management (OCRWM), which was established by the Nuclear Waste Policy Act of 1982 (NWPA, 42 U.S.C. 10101 et seq.) to dispose of highly radioactive waste from nuclear power plants and defense facilities. OCRWM had been developing a permanent nuclear waste repository at Yucca Mountain, NV, as specified by an NWPA amendment in 1987. Funding for OCWRM ended after FY2010, so the office has been closed and activities at the Yucca Mountain site halted.

The Obama Administration "has determined that developing the Yucca Mountain repository is not a workable option and the Nation needs a different solution for nuclear waste disposal," according to the DOE FY2011 budget justification. To develop alternative waste management strategies, the Administration established the Blue Ribbon Commission on America's Nuclear Future, which issued its final report to the Secretary of Energy on January 26, 2012.[66] The Blue Ribbon Commission recommended that future efforts to develop nuclear waste facilities follow a "consent based" approach and be carried out by a new organization, rather than DOE. The commission said the new nuclear waste entity should have "assured access" to the Nuclear Waste Fund, which holds fees collected from nuclear power plant operators to pay for waste disposal. Under NWPA, those funds cannot be spent without congressional appropriations.

DOE released its *Strategy for the Management and Disposal of Used Nuclear Fuel and High-Level Radioactive Waste* in January 2013 in response to the Blue Ribbon Commission report. The strategy calls for a pilot interim storage facility for spent fuel from closed nuclear reactors to open by 2021 and a larger storage facility, possibly at the same site, to open by 2025. A site for a permanent underground waste repository would be selected by 2026, and the repository would open by 2048. Storage and disposal sites would be selected by a new waste management organization through a consent-based process, as recommended by the Blue Ribbon Commission.[67]

With the dismantlement of OCRWM, DOE's Office of Nuclear Energy (NE) was given the responsibility to "lead all future waste management activities," according to the FY2011 budget justification. NE's Fuel Cycle R&D Program (discussed in the *Nuclear Energy* section above) includes funding under the Used Nuclear Fuel Disposition subprogram to begin implementing the DOE waste management strategy. DOE is seeking $60.0 million for the Used Fuel subprogram in FY2014, $2.1 million above the FY2012 funding level.

The House Appropriations Committee excoriated the Obama Administration's termination of the Yucca Mountain project as "blatant political maneuverings." The House bill would eliminate DOE's $60 million request to implement its new nuclear waste policy and add $25 million for Yucca Mountain. It would also authorize funding from the Nuclear Waste Fund to be transferred to the Nuclear Regulatory Commission for Yucca Mountain licensing.

---

[65] This section was prepared by Mark Holt.

[66] Blue Ribbon Commission on America's Nuclear Future, *Report to the Secretary of Energy*, January 2012, http://brc.gov/sites/default/files/documents/brc_finalreport_jan2012.pdf.

[67] DOE, *Strategy for the Management and Disposal of Used Nuclear Fuel and High-Level Radioactive Waste*, January 2013, http://energy.gov/sites/prod/files/ Strategy%20for%20the%20Management%20and%20Disposal%20of%20Used%20Nuclear%20Fuel%20and%20High %20Level%20Radioactive%20Waste.pdf.

The Senate Appropriations Committee approved the Administration's proposed funding level for Used Fuel and did not mention Yucca Mountain. The committee-passed bill includes a provision from the previous year that would authorize DOE to conduct a pilot program to develop one or more high level radioactive waste storage facilities, with the consent of state, local, and tribal governments.

The FY2014 budget request includes a proposal to change the nuclear waste funding system along the lines proposed by the Blue Ribbon Commission. Discretionary funding (annual appropriations by Congress) would continue to pay for "regular and recurring" expenses of the nuclear waste program. In the past, discretionary appropriations for the program have come from both the Nuclear Waste Fund, to pay for disposal of commercial reactor waste, and from the General Fund, to pay for defense waste disposal. Beginning in FY2017, under the Administration proposal, the discretionary appropriations would be supplemented by mandatory appropriations, first from incoming nuclear waste fee revenues and eventually from past fees and interest that have accumulated in the Waste Fund. If Congress enacted such mandatory appropriations, the specified funding would be automatically provided to the waste program without the need for annual congressional approval. Neither the House nor Senate bill included the proposed change.

DOE had filed a license application with the Nuclear Regulatory Commission (NRC) for the proposed Yucca Mountain repository in June 2008 but filed a motion to withdraw the application on March 3, 2010. An NRC licensing panel rejected DOE's withdrawal motion June 29, 2010, on the grounds that NWPA requires full consideration of the license application by NRC. The full NRC Commission deadlocked on the issue September 9, 2011, leaving the licensing panel's decision in place and prohibiting DOE from withdrawing the Yucca Mountain application. However, the commission ordered at the same time that the licensing process be halted because of "budgetary limitations."[68] No funding was provided in FY2012 or FY2013 or requested for FY2014 to continue Yucca Mountain licensing activities. However, the U.S. Court of Appeals for the District of Columbia Circuit ruled on August 13, 2013, that NRC must continue work on the Yucca Mountain license application as long as funding is available. The Court determined that NRC has at least $11.1 million in previously appropriated funds for that purpose.[69]

NWPA required DOE to begin taking waste from nuclear plant sites by January 31, 1998. Nuclear utilities, upset over DOE's failure to meet that deadline, have won two federal court decisions upholding the department's obligation to meet the deadline and to compensate utilities for any resulting damages. Utilities have also won several cases in the U.S. Court of Federal Claims. DOE estimates that liability payments would eventually exceed $20 billion if DOE were to begin removing waste from reactor sites by 2020, the previous target for opening Yucca Mountain.[70] (For more information, see CRS Report R42513, *U.S. Spent Nuclear Fuel Storage*, by James D. Werner; CRS Report RL33461, *Civilian Nuclear Waste Disposal*, by Mark Holt; and CRS Report R40996, *Contract Liability Arising from the Nuclear Waste Policy Act (NWPA) of 1982*, by Todd Garvey.)

---

[68] Nuclear Regulatory Commission, "In the Matter of U.S. Department of Energy (High-Level Waste Repository)," CLI-11-07, September 9, 2011, http://www.nrc.gov/reading-rm/doc-collections/commission/orders/2011/2011-07cli.pdf.

[69] U.S. Court of Appeals for the District of Columbia Circuit, *In re: Aiken County et al.*, No. 11-1271, writ of mandamus, August 13, 2013, http://www.cadc.uscourts.gov/internet/opinions nsf/BAE0CF34F762EBD985257BC6004DEB18/$file/11-1271-1451347.pdf.

[70] Ibid., p. 80.

Loan Guarantees and Direct Loans[71]

DOE's Loan Programs Office provides loan guarantees for projects that deploy specified energy technologies, as authorized by Title XVII of the Energy Policy Act of 2005 (EPACT05, P.L. 109-58), and direct loans for advanced vehicle manufacturing technologies. No funding for additional loans and loan guarantees was requested for FY2014. However, $48 million for loan guarantee administrative expenses, $10 million above FY2012, would be offset by fees. An additional $6 million was requested for administrative expenses for the vehicle manufacturing loan program, the same as FY2012. The House bill would limit the loan guarantee program's administrative expenses to $22 million, equal to CBO's estimated offset from fees, while the Senate Appropriations Committee recommended $42 million. Both the House bill and the Senate committee recommendation would provide the full $6 million Administration request for the vehicle manufacturing loan program.

Two major loan guarantee programs are currently administered by the DOE Loan Programs Office:

- *Section 1703 innovative clean energy technology loan guarantees.* Loan guarantees are provided for "new or significantly improved technologies," as compared to existing commercial technologies, that "avoid, reduce, or sequester" air pollutants and greenhouse gas emissions. Eligible technology categories include renewable energy, advanced fossil energy, advanced nuclear energy, energy efficiency, and pollution control.

- *Section 1705 renewable energy, electric transmission, and advanced biofuels loan guarantees.* Established by Section 406 of the American Recovery and Reinvestment Act (ARRA, P.L. P.L. 111-5), the Section 1705 program was designed as a temporary economic stimulus measure available through the end of FY2011. Unlike the Section 1703 program, which is limited to innovative technologies, loan guarantees are available to already-commercialized renewable energy and electric transmission technologies.

Title XVII allows DOE to provide loan guarantees for up to 80% of construction costs for eligible energy projects. Under such loan guarantee agreements, the federal government would repay all covered loans if the borrower defaulted. This would reduce the risk to lenders and allow them to provide financing at below-market interest rates. DOE currently has two conditional loan guarantee commitments pending under Section 1703, totaling $10.33 billion for nuclear power and nuclear fuel projects. Under Section 1705, final loan guarantees have been issued for 26 projects, totaling $16 billion.[72]

DOE's first loan guarantee under Section 1705 was issued in September 2009 to Solyndra Inc., a manufacturer of photovoltaic equipment. Solyndra's bankruptcy announcement on August 31, 2011, prompted strong congressional criticism of the Administration's management of the loan

---

[71] This section was prepared by Mark Holt. For more details on loan guarantees, see CRS Report R42152, *Loan Guarantees for Clean Energy Technologies: Goals, Concerns, and Policy Options*, by Phillip Brown.

[72] U.S. Department of Energy Loan Programs Office, "The Financing Force Behind America's Clean Energy Economy," https://lpo.energy.gov/?page_id=45. For a critique of the loan guarantee process, see U.S. Government Accountability Office, *DOE Loan Guarantees: Further Actions Are Needed to Improve Tracking and Review of Applications*, GAO-12-157, March 2012, http://www.gao.gov/products/GAO-12-157.

guarantee program.[73] Solyndra's DOE loan guarantee totaled $535 million, and the company's bankruptcy placed most or all of that amount at risk. (For details, see CRS Report R42058, *Market Dynamics That May Have Contributed to Solyndra's Bankruptcy*, by Phillip Brown.)

Subsidy Costs

Title XVII requires the estimated future government costs resulting from defaults on guaranteed loans to be covered up-front by appropriations or by payments from project sponsors (borrowers). These "subsidy costs" are calculated as the present value of the average possible future net costs to the government for each loan guarantee, on a case-by-case basis. If those calculations are accurate, the subsidy cost payments for all the guaranteed projects together should cover the future costs of the program. However, the Congressional Budget Office has predicted that the up-front subsidy cost payments will prove too low by at least 1% and is scoring bills accordingly.[74] As a result, appropriations bills that provide loan guarantee authorizations include an adjustment totaling 1% of the loan guarantee ceiling.

Subsidy costs for Section 1703 loan guarantees must usually be paid by project sponsors, because no appropriations for that program were provided before FY2011 (as described below). However, ARRA appropriated $6 billion to cover the subsidy costs of Section 1705 loan guarantees, so subsidy cost payments were not required from project sponsors under that program. However, $2 billion of Section 1705 subsidy cost appropriation was subsequently transferred to the "cash for clunkers" automobile trade-in program by P.L. 111-47, and another $1.5 billion was rescinded to help pay for the Education Jobs and Medicaid Assistance Act (P.L. 111-226), leaving $2.5 billion. Of the $2.5 billion available for subsidy costs, $1.9 billion was obligated by the end of FY2011.[75]

Authorized Loan Guarantee Amounts

Under the Federal Credit Reform Act (FCRA), federal loan guarantees cannot be provided without an authorized level in an appropriations act or an appropriation for the subsidy costs. Pursuant to FCRA, the FY2007 continuing resolution (P.L. 110-5) established an initial cap of $4 billion on loan guarantees under the Section 1703 program, without allocating that amount among the various eligible technologies. That authority has been amended and several times, to increase, cut, and/or further specify the authority. Currently, loan authority stands at $18.5 billion for nuclear loan guarantees, $4 billion for uranium enrichment, and $11.5 billion for non-nuclear projects.

Unobligated appropriations for subsidy cost payments under the Section 1705 loan guarantee program were no longer available after FY2011, as noted above. However, the FY2011 Continuing Appropriations Act provided $170 million, with no expiration, to pay subsidy costs for renewable energy and efficiency projects under the Section 1703 program. The act also

[73] Opening Statement of the Honorable Cliff Stearns, Chairman, Subcommittee on Oversight and Investigations. "Solyndra and the DOE Loan Guarantee Program," September 14, 2011, http://republicans.energycommerce house.gov/Media/file/Hearings/Oversight/091411/Stearns.pdf.

[74] Congressional Budget Office, *S. 1321, Energy Savings Act of 2007*, CBO Cost Estimate, Washington, DC, June 11, 2007, pp. 7-9, http://www.cbo.gov/ftpdocs/82xx/doc8206/s1321.pdf; and CBO, Fair-Value Accounting for Federal Credit Programs, Issue Brief, March 2012, http://www.cbo.gov/publication/43027.

[75] DOE Weekly Financial and Activity Report, September 30, 2011, http://www recovery.gov/transparency/agency/reporting/agency_reporting2.aspx?agency_code=89&dt=09/30/2011.

provided authority for up to $1.183 billion in loan guarantees for those renewable energy and efficiency projects, in addition to the $32.8 billion in Section 1703 authority remaining from earlier appropriations acts for all technologies. The additional loan guarantee authority and subsidy cost appropriation provided by the FY2011 Continuing Appropriations Act is available to projects that applied under the expiring Section 1705 before February 24, 2011.

Following is a summary of the various elements of the current DOE loan guarantee program, as modified by the FY2011 Continuing Appropriations Act (CR):

- $8.3 billion ceiling in CR on non-nuclear technologies under Section 1703, reduced from ceilings set in FY2009.

- $2 billion for unspecified projects from FY2007 under Section 1703, not affected by CR.

- $18.5 billion ceiling for nuclear power plants ($8.3 billion conditionally committed).

- $4 billion allocated for loan guarantees for uranium enrichment plants ($2 billion conditionally committed).

- $1.183 billion ceiling for renewable energy and energy efficiency projects under Section 1703, in addition to other ceiling amounts, which can include pending applications under Section 1705.

- An appropriation of $170 million for subsidy costs for renewable energy and energy efficiency loan guarantees under Section 1703. If the subsidy costs averaged 10% of the loan guarantees, this funding could support loan guarantees totaling $1.7 billion.

- $2.5 billion for Section 1705 subsidy costs appropriated by ARRA. As noted above, about $1.9 billion of this funding was used to pay the subsidy costs for $16 billion in loan guarantees with final commitments under Section 1705, for which the deadline was September 30, 2011.[76] Therefore, the remainder is not currently available to the program.

Advanced Technology Vehicle Manufacturing Loans

DOE also administers the Advanced Technology Vehicles Manufacturing (ATVM) Loan Program established by the Energy Independence and Security Act of 2007 (P.L. 110-140).[77] The FY2009 Continuing Resolution appropriated $7.5 billion to allow DOE to issue up to $25 billion in direct loans. The program was designed to provide loans to eligible automobile manufacturers and parts suppliers for making investments in their plant capacity to produce vehicles with improved fuel economy. Along with the EPACT loan guarantee programs, the ATVM Loan Program is administered by the DOE Loan Programs Office. DOE reports that five ATVM loans have been issued, totaling $8.4 billion.[78]

---

[76] DOE Loan Programs Office, "Our Projects," http://lpo.energy.gov/our-projects.

[77] For more details, see CRS Report R42064, *The Advanced Technology Vehicles Manufacturing (ATVM) Loan Program: Status and Issues*, by Brent D. Yacobucci and Bill Canis.

[78] U.S. Department of Energy Loan Programs Office, "The Financing Force Behind America's Clean Energy Economy," https://lpo.energy.gov/?page_id=45.

Nuclear Weapons Stockpile Stewardship[79]

Congress established the Stockpile Stewardship Program in the FY1994 National Defense Authorization Act (P.L. 103-160). The goal of the program, as amended by the FY2010 National Defense Authorization Act (P.L. 111-84, §3111), is to ensure "that the nuclear weapons stockpile is safe, secure, and reliable without the use of underground nuclear weapons testing." The program is operated by the National Nuclear Security Administration (NNSA), a semiautonomous agency within DOE that Congress established in the FY2000 National Defense Authorization Act (P.L. 106-65, Title XXXII).

Stockpile stewardship consists of all activities in NNSA's Weapons Activities account, as described below. **Table 12** presents Weapons Activities funding. NNSA manages two programs outside of that account: Defense Nuclear Nonproliferation, discussed later in this report, and Naval Reactors.

Most stewardship activities take place at the nuclear weapons complex (the "complex"), which consists of three laboratories (Los Alamos National Laboratory, NM; Lawrence Livermore National Laboratory, CA; and Sandia National Laboratories, NM and CA); four production sites (Kansas City Plant, MO; Pantex Plant, TX; Savannah River Site, SC; and Y-12 National Security Complex, TN); and the Nevada National Security Site (formerly Nevada Test Site). NNSA manages and sets policy for the complex; contractors to NNSA operate the eight sites.

Table 12. Funding for Weapons Activities, FY2011-FY2014

($ millions)

Program	FY2013 Approp.[a]	FY2014 Request	FY2014 House	FY2014 Senate	FY2014 Conf.
DSW	2,116.4	2428.5	2718.4	2258.5	
Campaigns	1,692.2	1710.9	1626.1	1847.4	
RTBF[b]	2,144.3	0	1909.7	0	
Nuclear Programs	0.0	744.5	0	688.0	
Site Stewardship	79.1	1706.0	154.8	0	
Site Ops & Maint	0.0	0	0	1535.9	
Other[c]	1,542.9	1,278.5	1266.1	1538.7	
Total	**7,574.9**	**7,868.4**	**7,675.0**	**7,868.4**	

Source: FY2014 Budget Request; H.Rept. 113-135; S.Rept. 113-47.

Notes: Details may not add to totals due to rounding. DSW: Directed Stockpile Work; RTBF: Readiness in Technical Base and Facilities.

a. Source: H.Rept. 113-135. Figures do not reflect the March 1, 2013, sequester of funds under P.L. 112-25.

b. For FY2014, NNSA eliminated RTBF and split its functions between Nuclear Programs (a new program) and Site Stewardship. Also for FY2014, NNSA shifted Nuclear Counterterrorism Incident Response and National Security Applications from Weapons Activities to Defense Nuclear Nonproliferation. See text for further details.

---

[79] This section was prepared by Jonathan Medalia.

c. For FY2012, "other" includes Secure Transportation Asset, Nuclear Counterterrorism Incident Response, Defense Nuclear Security, Facilities and Infrastructure Recapitalization Program, Cyber Security, National Security Applications, and Legacy Contractor Pensions. For FY2014, "other" includes Secure Transportation Asset, Defense Nuclear Security, Information Technology and Cyber Security (House and Senate Appropriations Committees), Nuclear Counterterrorism Incident Response (Senate Appropriations Committee), NNSA CIO Activities (request), Legacy Contractor Pensions, and use of prior year balances.

Table 13. Weapons Activities: FY2014 Request and FY2015-FY2018 Plan

($ millions, except bottom row: $ billions)

	FY2014	FY2015	FY2016	FY2017	FY2018
DSW	2,428.5	2,539.7	2,586.3	2,732.4	3.045.5
Campaigns	1,710.9	1,918.6	1,948.6	1,911,3	1,924.1
Nuclear Programs	744.5	994.1	1,191.6	1,208.5	1,333.2
Site Stewardship	1,706.0	1,745.4	1,729.2	1,775.7	1,705.6
Other[a]	1,278.5	1,351.9	1,329.7	1,304.8	1,284.4
Total	**7,868.4**	**8,549.7**	**8,785.4**	**8,932.8**	**9,292.9**
Nov. 2010 "1251 report" projection	**8.4**	**8.7**	**8.9**	**8.9-9.0**	**9.2-9.3**

Source: FY2014 NNSA Budget Request for rows through Total; bottom row, U.S. White House. "November 2010 Update to the National Defense Authorization Act of FY2010 Section 1251 Report: New START Treaty Framework and Nuclear Force Structure Plans," p. 9, http://www.lasg.org/CMRR/Sect1251_update_17Nov2010.pdf.

Notes: Details may not add to totals due to rounding. DSW: Directed Stockpile Work.

a. "Other" includes Secure Transportation Asset, Defense Nuclear Security, Cyber Security, NNSA CIO Activities, and Legacy Contractor Pensions. For FY2014, Other also includes use of prior year balances.

NNSA proposed many changes to the budget structure for FY2014. It would create an Office of Infrastructure and Operations to be the landlord of the nuclear weapons complex sites, with program offices as tenants. As a result, NNSA proposed to eliminate Readiness in Technical Base and Facilities and split its functions between a greatly increased Site Stewardship program and a new Nuclear Programs, as described below. NNSA also proposed moving Nuclear Counterterrorism Incident Response and National Security Applications to Defense Nuclear Nonproliferation, an appropriations account separate from Weapons Activities.

Nuclear Weapons Complex Reconfiguration

Although the nuclear weapons complex currently consists of eight sites, it was much larger during the Cold War in terms of number of sites and personnel. Despite the post-Cold War reductions, many in Congress have for years wanted the complex to change further, in various ways: fewer personnel, greater efficiency, smaller footprint at each site, increased security, and the like. After numerous exchanges between DOE and the appropriating and authorizing committees, such issues still remain.

According to a White House document of May 2010, the President provided Congress with a classified report (the "1251 report") required by the FY2010 National Defense Authorization Act,

Section 1251, "on the comprehensive plan to: (1) maintain delivery platforms [that is, bombers, missiles, and submarines that deliver nuclear weapons]; (2) sustain a safe, secure, and reliable U.S. nuclear weapons stockpile; and (3) modernize the nuclear weapons complex."[80] According to that document, "the Administration intends to invest $80 billion in the next decade to sustain and modernize the nuclear weapons complex." The Administration submitted a revised Section 1251 report in November 2010, projecting weapons stockpile and infrastructure costs for FY2011-FY2020 at between $85.4 billion and $86.2 billion. Its estimate for FY2013 was $7.9 billion.

For FY2013, the Administration requested $7,577.3 million for Weapons Activities, less than the amount in the November 2010 1251 report. The request brought criticism from some Members, but the House and Senate Appropriations Committees recommended the amount requested. The Consolidated and Further Continuing Appropriations Act for FY2013 (P.L. 113-6) funded Weapons Activities at a rate equivalent to an annual $7,577.3 million, the amount requested by the Administration for FY2013. However, the Budget Control Act of 2011 (P.L. 112-25) mandated a sequester unless Congress took certain actions. Since Congress did not take those actions, the Office of Management and Budget calculated sequester amounts for programs, projects, and activities; the amount for Weapons Activities was $604 million.[81] However, NNSA has not provided CRS with post-sequester figures for each project, program, and activity; accordingly, *the FY2013 figures used in the balance of this section are pre-sequester amounts.*

In contrast to the FY2013 request, the FY2014 request included out-year figures. As **Table 13** shows, the projected Weapons Activities requests for FY2015-FY2018 are within 2% of the amounts projected in the November 2010 1251 report update.

Directed Stockpile Work (DSW)

This program involves work directly on nuclear weapons in the stockpile, such as monitoring their condition; maintaining them through repairs, refurbishment, life extension, and modifications; conducting R&D in support of specific warheads; and dismantlement. Specific items under DSW include the following:

Life Extension Programs (LEPs). These programs aim to extend the life of existing warheads through design, certification, manufacture, and replacement of components. An LEP for the B61 mods 7 and 11 bombs was completed in FY2009. (A "mod" is a modification or version of a bomb or warhead type.) An LEP for the W76 warhead for the Trident II submarine-launched ballistic missile is ongoing, as is an LEP for the B61 mod 12. The FY2013 appropriation was $237.3 million for the W76 LEP and $352.7 million for the B61 LEP.

The FY2014 request for Life Extension Programs (which NNSA proposed renaming Life Extension Programs and Major Alterations), contains four elements.

---

[80] U.S. White House. "The New START Treaty—Maintaining a Strong Nuclear Deterrent," fact sheet, May 13, 2010, http://www.america.gov/st/texttrans-english/2010/May/20100514114003xjsnommis0.6300318.html.

[81] U.S. Executive Office of the President. Office of Management and Budget. OMB Report to the Congress on the Joint Committee Sequestration for Fiscal Year 2013, March 1, 2013, p. 22, http://www.whitehouse.gov/sites/default/files/omb/assets/legislative_reports/fy13ombjcsequestrationreport.pdf. For an extended description of the debate over funding the weapons program, see CRS Report R42498, *Energy and Water Development: FY2013 Appropriations*, coordinated by Carl E. Behrens.

- The request for the B61-12 LEP is $537.0 million to continue development engineering and ramp up system development testing. NNSA's plan is to make the first production unit in FY2019. The House Appropriations Committee recommended $560.7 million; the increase was to address a funding gap resulting from "efficiencies" in the program that NNSA did not specify. The Senate Appropriations Committee recommended $369.0 million. It expressed concern that the LEP option proposed "is not the lowest cost, lowest risk option that meets military requirements and replaces aging components before they affect weapon performance."

- NNSA requests $235.4 million for the W76-1 LEP. NNSA intends to complete W76-1 production by FY2019. The House Appropriations Committee recommended $248.5 million. The increase addressed several issues: "inadequately fund[ed] activities that are essential to meet production needs of the W76," a proposed reduction in the number of W76s, and estimated cost efficiencies that "are unlikely to be realized." The Senate Appropriations Committee recommended the requested amount.

- NNSA requests $72.7 million for the W78/W88-1 LEP. The W78 is a warhead for a land-based intercontinental ballistic missile, while the W88 is a warhead for a submarine-launched ballistic missile. The LEP would produce a common interoperable warhead. The House Appropriations Committee recommended $50.0 million. This amount funds a study of W78 life extension and "permits continued consideration of an integrated warhead [i.e., the W78/W88-1], but only as part of a continued study of alternatives." The Senate Appropriations Committee recommended the requested amount. It expressed concern about the cost for the LEP, which NNSA projects at $14 billion, and directed NNSA not to preclude a separate LEP for the W78.

- NNSA requests $169.5 million for the W88 Alteration (Alt) 370, which includes development engineering to support replacement of the arming, fusing, and firing system and other components, with a first production unit in FY2019. The House and Senate Appropriations Committees recommended the requested amount.

Stockpile Systems. This program involves routine maintenance, replacement of limited-life components, surveillance, assessment, and the like for all weapon types in the stockpile. For FY2013, the program was funded at $563.9 million. For 2014, the W78/W88 study and the Alt 370 have advanced sufficiently to move to Life Extension Programs. As a result, Stockpile Systems funding requested declined to $454.5 million for FY2014. The House Appropriations Committee recommended the requested amount. The Senate Appropriations Committee recommended $282.8 million. It provided a lump sum rather than a weapon-by-weapon amount, and moved funds requested under Stockpile Systems for warhead surveillance to a new Surveillance budget line, for which it recommended $234.6 million.

Weapons Dismantlement and Disposition (WDD). The number of warheads has fallen sharply since the end of the Cold War, and continues to decline. WDD involves interim storage of warheads to be dismantled; dismantlement; and disposition (i.e., storing or eliminating warhead components and materials). The FY2013 appropriation was $44.3 million, and the FY2014 request is $49.3 million. The House Appropriations Committee recommended $55.3 million, and stated, "NNSA continues to cut funding for dismantlement, despite a clear requirement to continue to dismantle warheads, sustain production line capacity, and harvest materials for recycling to meet stockpile needs." The Senate Appropriations Committee recommended $56.0

million, with the increase to be used to "reduce the backlog in dispositioning nuclear components from dismantled nuclear warheads."

Stockpile Services. This category includes Production Support; R&D Support; R&D Certification and Safety; Management, Technology, and Production; and Plutonium Infrastructure Sustainment. NNSA states, "Stockpile Services provides the foundation for the production capability and capacity within the nuclear security enterprise. All enduring systems, LEPs, and dismantlements rely on Stockpile Services to provide the base development, production and logistics capability needed to meet program requirements. In addition, Stockpile Services funds research, development and production activities that support two or more weapons-types, and work that is not identified or allocated to a specific weapon-type." The FY2013 appropriation provided $917.8 million. The FY2014 request was $910.2 million. The House Appropriations Committee recommended $1,180.0 million, with reductions to large requested increases in certification on grounds that NNSA has not demonstrated the need for such increases, and increases due to inclusion in Stockpile Services of certain funds requested elsewhere in the budget. The Senate Appropriations Committee recommended $838.5 million and moved several programs into or out of Stockpile Services.

Campaigns

These are "multi-year, multi-functional efforts" that "provide specialized scientific knowledge and technical support to the directed stockpile work on the nuclear weapons stockpile." Many campaigns have significance for policy decisions. For example, the Science Campaign's goals include improving the ability to assess warhead performance without nuclear testing, improving readiness to conduct nuclear tests should the need arise, and maintaining the scientific infrastructure of the nuclear weapons laboratories. Campaigns also fund some large experimental facilities, such as the National Ignition Facility at Lawrence Livermore National Laboratory. The FY2013 and FY2014 requests included five campaigns:

Science Campaign. The FY2013 appropriation was $349.2 million; the FY2014 request is $397.9 million. Within this campaign, the largest increases went to (1) Advanced Certification, which among other things conducts experiments to help "select technologies for re-use of existing pits in LEP designs using Insensitive High Explosive (IHE)";[82] Primary Assessment Technologies, which among other things "address[es] plutonium aging and material compatibility issues associated with pit re-use"; and Dynamic Materials Properties, which among other things will conduct "increased experimental efforts on plutonium as a function of age in existing pits intended for reuse" because they "are required in order to enable upcoming LEPs without the need to build significant numbers of new pits." For FY2014, the House Appropriations Committee recommended the requested amount. The Senate Appropriations Committee recommended $374.7 million.

Engineering Campaign. This campaign "funds activities that assess and improve fielded nuclear and non-nuclear engineering components without further underground testing." For FY2013, $138.8 million was appropriated; the FY2014 request is $149.9 million. The House Appropriations Committee recommended the requested amount. The Senate Appropriations Committee recommended $90.0 million, and recommended moving certain funds from this campaign to a new Technology Maturation Campaign.

---

[82] IHE is a type of explosive that is less likely to detonate under certain accident conditions.

Inertial Confinement Fusion Ignition and High Yield Campaign. This campaign is developing the tools to create extremely high temperatures and pressures in the laboratory—approaching those of a nuclear explosion—to support weapons-related research and to attract scientific talent to the Stockpile Stewardship Program. NNSA states, "Virtually all of the energy from a nuclear weapon is generated while in the high energy density (HED) state. High-energy density physics (HEDP) experiments conducted at ICF facilities are required to validate the advanced theoretical models used to assess and certify the stockpile without nuclear testing. The National Ignition Facility (NIF) extends HEDP experiments to include access to thermonuclear burn conditions in the laboratory, a unique and unprecedented scientific achievement."

The centerpiece of this campaign is NIF, the world's largest laser. While NIF was controversial in Congress for many years and had significant cost growth and technical problems, controversy waned as the program progressed. The facility was dedicated in May 2009.[83] Between February 20, 2011, and March 20, 2011, NIF personnel conducted 34 "successful target shots ... in support of HEDSS [High Energy Density Stockpile Stewardship]."[84] In 2011, personnel conducted a total of 283 NIF shots of all types.[85]

However, as experiments proceeded, the prospect that NIF would soon achieve fusion ignition began to fade. The House Appropriations Committee in its FY2012 report stated, "the considerable costs [for NIF] will not have been warranted if the only role the National Ignition Facility (NIF) serves is that of an expensive platform for routine high energy density physics experiments." The Senate Appropriations Committee expressed its concern over the prospects of NIF achieving ignition by the end of FY2012 and directed NNSA to establish an advisory committee on this and related topics.

For FY2013, the appropriation for this campaign was $485.5 million. The FY2014 request was $401.0 million. The largest decreases are for Diagnostics, Cryogenics, and Experimental Support, reflecting a reduction in facility operations, and for Facility Operations and Target Production, reflecting a reduction in shot rate at NIF and elimination of support for experiments by external users at NIF and a related facility. The House Appropriations Committee recommended $514.0 million. The increase resulted because NNSA had requested $113.0 million for NIF operations in another budget category (Site Stewardship); by moving those funds to this campaign, the committee "consolidates total funding for NIF facility operations within Campaigns." The Senate Appropriations Committee recommended $528.4 million, including moving $113.3 million for NIF operations from Site Stewardship to Facility Operations and Target Production.

Advanced Simulation and Computing (ASC) Campaign. This campaign develops computation-based models of nuclear weapons that integrate data from other campaigns, past test data, laboratory experiments, and elsewhere to create what NNSA calls "the computational surrogate for nuclear testing to determine weapon behavior." In addition, "ASC plays an important role in supporting nonproliferation, emergency response, nuclear forensics and attribution activities." Some analysts doubt that simulation can be relied upon to provide the

---

[83] Lawrence Livermore National Laboratory, "Dedication of World's Largest Laser Marks the Dawn of a New Era," press release, May 29, 2009, https://publicaffairs.llnl.gov/news/news_releases/2009/NR-09-05-05 html.

[84] "A Banner Month for NIF High Energy Density (HED) Experiments," *Project Status—2011, March*, Lawrence Livermore National Laboratory, https://lasers.llnl.gov/newsroom/project_status/2011/march.php.

[85] Lawrence Livermore National Laboratory, "Project Status—2011, December," https://lasers.llnl.gov/newsroom/project_status/2011/december.php.

confidence needed to certify the safety, security, and reliability of warheads, and advocate a return to testing. The campaign includes funds for hardware and operations as well as for software. For FY2013, the appropriation was $593.3 million; the FY2014 request was $564.3 million. The House Appropriations Committee recommended the requested amount. The Senate Appropriations Committee recommended $600.6 million, of which $69.0 million would be used for the exascale initiative, which is intended to lead to more-capable supercomputers.

Readiness Campaign. This campaign "operates the capability for producing tritium to maintain the national inventory needed for the nuclear weapons stockpile." The FY2013 appropriation was $125.3 million. The FY2014 request increased to $197.8 million. Tritium Readiness increased to $91.7 million because of "cost premiums for enrichment of unobligated reactor fuel" and "preparations for continued increases in production to meet mission requirements." Nonnuclear Readiness funds were realigned to a new subprogram, Component Manufacturing Development, "to restore the full capability to mature production processes and technologies." The House Appropriations Committee recommended no funds for this campaign, providing funds for programs in this campaign under Directed Stockpile Work "since those activities directly support stockpile production needs." The Senate Appropriations Committee recommended replacing the Readiness Campaign with the Technology Maturation Campaign, and recommended $253.7 million for the latter, which includes funds from Stockpile Services and the Engineering and Readiness Campaigns while moving funds for tritium activities to Stockpile Services.

Readiness in Technical Base and Facilities (RTBF)

This program funds infrastructure and operations at nuclear weapons complex sites. For FY2013, the appropriation was $2,144.3 million. NNSA would abolish this program in its FY2014 request, transferring its programs to the newly created Nuclear Programs and the much-expanded Site Stewardship. These two programs are discussed below; for comparison, the total FY2014 request for them is $2,450.5 million.

RTBF had several subprograms. The largest was Operations of Facilities (FY2013 appropriated, $1,419.5 million). The second largest was Construction (FY2013 appropriated, $441.5 million).

Perhaps the most controversial activity in the Weapons Activities account was the Chemistry and Metallurgy Research Facility Replacement (CMRR) project at Los Alamos National Laboratory. The project involves two buildings, the Radiation Laboratory/Utility/Office Building (RLUOB), which was completed in 2009, and the Nuclear Facility (NF), which has been designed but not built. CMRR would replace the Chemistry and Metallurgy Research (CMR) building, most of which was built in 1952. Among other things, CMR houses research into plutonium and supports pit production at Los Alamos, such as by conducting analytical chemistry procedures to monitor the quality of plutonium at various stages during the manufacture of a pit. Since 2005, cost estimates for CMRR increased several-fold, and some critics argue that it is not necessary. For FY2012, NNSA requested $300 million for CMRR but the conference report directed that "no construction activities are funded for the CMRR-Nuclear Facility during fiscal year 2012."

NNSA requested no funds for FY2013 or FY2014 for CMRR. According to the FY2013 request justification,

> NNSA has determined, in consultation with the national laboratories, that existing infrastructure in the nuclear complex has the inherent capacity to provide adequate support for plutonium chemistry, plutonium physics, and special nuclear materials. NNSA proposes

deferring CMRR Nuclear Facility construction for at least five years. Studies are ongoing to determine long-term requirements. Instead of the CMRR Nuclear Facility, NNSA will maximize use of existing facilities and relocate some nuclear materials. Estimated cost avoidance from FY 2013 to FY 2017 totals approximately $1.8 billion.

The House and Senate Appropriations Committees recommended no funds for CMRR-NF for FY2014. Meanwhile, NNSA continues to explore a strategy for producing pits.

Another project, the Uranium Processing Facility (UPF), was intended to replace old facilities at the Y-12 National Security Complex, some of which dated back to World War II. It would conduct operations involving enriched uranium for nuclear weapons and naval reactors. It would also conduct downblending of enriched uranium (i.e., reducing the fraction of fissile uranium-235 and increasing the fraction of non-fissile uranium-238) to make it unusable for weapons in support of nuclear nonproliferation. The FY2013 appropriation was $340.0 million. For FY2014, NNSA renamed UPF the Uranium Capabilities Replacement Project and requested $325.8 million for it. The House Appropriations Committee recommended the requested amount, but expressed concern about "the steep escalation in costs to complete design of the facility." The Senate Appropriations Committee recommended the requested amount, while expressing concern about project management. "Most recently, a space fit issue that required raising the roof of the building by 13 feet to fit critical equipment resulted in more than $500,000,000 in additional costs."

Nuclear Programs

This program focuses on processing and managing Special Nuclear Materials (i.e., uranium highly enriched in isotope 235 and plutonium). Its goals are to supply required quantities of these materials; recycle, recover, and store these materials; and sustain program skills. It has three elements. (1) Nuclear Operations Capability, which among other things includes Plutonium Metal Reprocessing, "a new funding line to receive pits from Pantex and process plutonium to establish an inventory of purified metal alloy that will support manufacturing 30 pits per year and help mitigate the risk of the decision to defer the construction" of CMRR-NF; (2) Capabilities Based Investments, which seek to sustain capabilities supporting weapons activities; and (3) Construction. The FY2014 request for this new program is $744.5 million.

The House Appropriations Committee was sharply critical of NNSA's use of this new budget category. It would not "consider changing the congressional budget structure ... for bureaucratic reorganizations and not for new funding lines that are poorly justified." Accordingly, it "selectively funded the activities requested under Nuclear Programs using the existing budget structure." The Senate Appropriations Committee "has renamed the two new accounts that encompass previous RTBF functions to provide greater clarity: (1) Nuclear Operations and Capital Construction and (2) Site Operations and Maintenance." The committee recommended $688.0 million for Nuclear Operations and Capital Construction, of which $439.0 million is for major capital construction projects as requested.

Site Stewardship

The FY2013 appropriation for this program was $79.1 million. The FY2014 budget request would expand this program to $1,706.0 million and restructure its mission. Almost all—$1,660.8 million, or 97.4%—of Site Stewardship would be for Enterprise Infrastructure, the major elements of which were Site Operations ($1,112.5 million requested), Site Support ($109.6 million requested to fund nuclear safety, R&D and waste management, among other things), and

Sustainment ($433.8 million requested to fund some of NNSA's direct maintenance activities). Four other programs in Site Stewardship had requests of less than $18 million.

The House Appropriations Committee recommended $154.8 million for Site Stewardship, but declined to fund certain programs under it. "The reduction below the request is due to continued funding of infrastructure under Readiness in Technical Base and Facilities. The NNSA should not request funding for site facility operations, maintenance, or recapitalization within Site Stewardship." The Senate Appropriations Committee did not provide funds under Site Stewardship, instead providing most of the requested funds, $1,535.9 million, under Site Operations and Maintenance.

Other Programs

Weapons Activities includes several smaller programs in addition to DSW, Campaigns, Nuclear Programs, and Site Stewardship. Among them:

Secure Transportation Asset provides for safe and secure transport of nuclear weapons, components, and materials. It includes special vehicles for this purpose, communications and other supporting infrastructure, and threat response. For FY2013, the appropriation was $219.1 million. The FY2014 request is $219.2 million. The House and Senate Appropriations Committees recommended the requested amount.

Nuclear Counterterrorism Incident Response "responds to and mitigates nuclear and radiological incidents worldwide and has a lead role in defending the Nation from the threat of nuclear terrorism." The FY2013 appropriation was $253.0 million. For FY2014, NNSA transferred this program to Defense Nuclear Nonproliferation "to align all NNSA funding for reducing global nuclear dangers in one appropriation," and the House Appropriations Committee did not consider funding for it under Weapons Activities. In contrast, the Senate Appropriations Committee recommended $260.2 million for this program, and did not approve transferring this account to Defense Nuclear Nonproliferation.

Defense Nuclear Security provides operations, maintenance, and construction funds for protective forces, physical security systems, personnel security, and the like. It "provides protection from a full spectrum of threats, especially terrorism, for NNSA personnel, facilities, nuclear weapons, and information." The FY2013 appropriation was $724.5 million. Prior to FY2014, this program was a component of Safeguards and Security. In the FY2014 request, NNSA abolished Safeguards and Security and made Defense Nuclear Security a standalone program. The FY2014 request is $679.0 million, of which $14.0 million is for a security upgrade at the Device Assembly Facility (DAF) in the Nevada National Security Site. NNSA, in its request, noted that various security enhancements had been taken or were underway in response to the July 2012 security breach at Y-12. The House Appropriations Committee recommended $665.0 million. It noted that some of the reduction from the FY2013 level was due to removal of special nuclear material from Lawrence Livermore National Laboratory, and deferred funding for the DAF upgrade. The Senate Appropriations Committee recommended the requested amount.

NNSA CIO [Chief Information Officer] Activities was a new program for FY2013 that sought to consolidate cyber security and information technology programs. Elements included cyber security, enterprise secure computing, and Federal Unclassified Information Technology. The latter will provide "commodity computing infrastructure" that will support a "shift from a traditional, costly desktop support model to a cloud-provisioned virtualized desktop-based solution." The FY2014 request for NNSA CIO Activities is $148.4 million. The House Appropriations Committee recommended $150.0 million and renamed the budget line Information Technology and Cyber Security "to more clearly describe the purposes for which the funds may be used." The Senate Appropriations Committee recommended the requested amount and also renamed the budget line Information Technology and Cyber Security.

The **National Security Applications** program is directed toward "national security science, technology and engineering." For FY2014, NNSA transferred activities funded by National Security Applications from Weapons Activities to Defense Nuclear Nonproliferation.

Legacy Contractor Pensions: For many decades, the University of California (UC) operated Los Alamos and Lawrence Livermore National Laboratories. Since laboratory employees were UC employees, they could participate in the university's pension plan. When the two labs were privatized, the contracts between DOE and the laboratory operators included provisions that in effect mirrored the pension that lab staff who were UC employees when the labs were privatized would have received had the labs remained with UC. These pensions were larger than those provided to employees hired after privatization. To make up the difference, NNSA paid into the pension plan for the UC employees. For Weapons Activities, the FY2013 appropriation for this payment was $185.0 million, and the FY2014 request is $279.6 million. (NNSA requested an additional amount for this purpose under Defense Nuclear Nonproliferation.) The House Appropriations Committee recommended the amount requested, but noted its concern "about the continually escalating costs of contractor pensions and other postretirement benefits and their impacts on programmatic activities." The Senate Appropriations Committee recommended the amount requested.

Nonproliferation and National Security Programs[86]

DOE's nonproliferation and national security programs provide technical capabilities to support U.S. efforts to prevent, detect, and counter the spread of nuclear weapons worldwide. These nonproliferation and national security programs are included in the National Nuclear Security Administration (NNSA).

---

[86] This section was prepared by Carl E. Behrens.

Table 14. DOE Defense Nuclear Nonproliferation Programs

($ millions)

Program	FY2013a Approp.	FY2014 Request	House	Senate	Conf.
Nonproliferation and Verification R&D	$356.2	$388.8	$388.8	$408.8	
Domestic Uranium Enrichment R&D	0.0	0.0	0.0	0.0	
Nonproliferation and International Security	155.3	141.7	128.7	128.0	
International Materials Protection and Control (IMPC)	571.6	369.6	369.6	419.6	
Fissile Materials Disposition	658.4	502.6	502.6	669.2	
Global Threat Reduction Initiative	500.0	424.5	408.3	497.5	
Legacy Contractor Pensions	55.8	93.7	93.7	93.7	
Nuclear Counterterrorism Incident Response	0.0	181.3	180.0	0.0	
Counterterrorism and Counterproliferation	0.0	74.7	65.0	0.0	
Rescissions and Use of Prior Year Funds	0.0	-36.7	-36.7	-36.7	
Total	**2,434.3**	**2,140.1**	**2,100.0**	**2,180.1**	

Source: FY2014 budget request; H.Rept. 113-135; S.Rept. 113-47.

Notes: Numbers may not add due to rounding.

a. Source: H.Rept. 113-135. Figures do not reflect the March 1, 2013, sequester of funds under P.L. 112-25.

Funding for these programs in FY2013 was $2,434.3 million. The request for FY2014 was $2,140.1 million, but that total includes two programs that the Administration proposes transferring from the Weapons Activities program: the Nuclear Counterterrorism Incident Response program and the Counterterrorism and Counterproliferation program. Without those two activities, the Nuclear Nonproliferation program request would be $1,884.2 million.

The Nonproliferation and Verification R&D program was funded at $356.2 million for FY2013. The request for FY2014 was $388.8 million. The Administration proposed renaming the program Defense Nuclear Nonproliferation R&D. The House bill would fund the program at the requested level. The Senate Appropriations Committee recommended $408.8 million.

Nonproliferation and International Security programs include international safeguards, export controls, and treaties and agreements. The FY2014 request for these programs was $141.7 million, compared with $155.3 million appropriated for FY2013. The House bill would appropriate $128.7 million; the Senate committee recommended $128.0 million.

International Materials Protection and Control (IMP&C), which is concerned with reducing the threat posed by unsecured Russian weapons and weapons-usable material, was funded at $571.6 million in FY2013; the FY2014 request was $369.6 million. The decrease, according to DOE's budget justification document, reflects a shift "to a sustainability phase with the Russian Federation" in which "security costs are increasingly transitioned to the Russian side." It also includes a reduction in the so-called Second Line of Defense Activities, mostly border and port detection programs, by $122 million, while the programs were under a strategic review. The House bill would appropriate the requested amount. The Senate bill would increase the funding to $419.7 million.

The goal of the Fissile Materials Disposition (FMD) program is disposal of U.S. surplus weapons plutonium by converting it into fuel for commercial power reactors, and a similar program in Russia. The U.S. side of the program originally included construction of three projects at Savannah River, SC: a facility to fabricate "mixed-oxide" (MOX) reactor fuel; a pit disassembly and conversion facility (PDCF), and a waste solidification facility. However, controversy developed over whether the pit disassembly project is necessary. The FY2012 request for the Fissile Materials Disposition program was $892.2 million, including $172 million for the PDCF, but the final bill appropriated $685.4 million for the program, and included no funding for the PDCF project, because, the conference report stated, "NNSA has not completed a study of alternatives or a conceptual design report with a cost and schedule estimate."

The FY2013 request for FMD programs was $921.3 million. No funding was asked for the PDCF; NNSA said it would use existing facilities for pit disassembly. The waste solidification facility was completed and no further funding was requested. The major cause of the increase was the planned cold start-up of the MOX facility. However, no funding increase for the MOX project was included in the FY2013 continuing resolution, and the start-up was delayed. The actual FY2013 MOX appropriation was $435.2 million; the total FMD appropriation was $685.4 million. In the meantime estimated total cost for the facility was increased from $4.8 billion to $7.7 billion, in part to expand its capability to carry out the functions of the cancelled PDCF plant.

In its FY2014 budget request, NNSA decided to slow down completion of the MOX plant, and begin a process of "evaluating alternatives for a new and affordable plutonium disposition strategy." It asked for a total of $502.6 million for FMD programs, including $320 million for the MOX plant. The House bill would appropriate the requested amount, but the House Appropriations Committee report said no additional funding would be provided to study alternatives to the MOX plant, since NNSA had not submitted any alternatives that had not been "exhaustively studied" or would likely cost less. The Senate Appropriations Committee rejected the pause in MOX construction, funding the facility at $430.6 million and total FMD programs at $669.2 million.

The Global Threat Reduction Initiative is aimed at converting research reactors around the world from using highly enriched uranium, removing and disposing of excess nuclear materials, and protecting nuclear materials from theft or sabotage. The FY2013 appropriation for this program was $500.0 million. The FY2014 request was $424.5 million. The House bill would appropriate $408.3 million. The Senate committee recommended $497.5 million.

Cleanup of Former Nuclear Weapons Production Facilities and Civilian Nuclear Energy Research Facilities[87]

The development and production of nuclear weapons for national defense purposes for over half a century since the beginning of the Manhattan Project resulted in a legacy of wastes and contamination that continues to present substantial challenges today. In 1989, DOE established what is now the Office of Environmental Management to consolidate its responsibilities for the cleanup of former nuclear weapons production facilities that had been administered under multiple offices.[88] These cleanup efforts are broad in scope and include the disposal of large quantities of radioactive and other hazardous wastes generated over decades; management and disposal of surplus nuclear materials; remediation of extensive contamination in soil and groundwater; decontamination and decommissioning of excess buildings and facilities; and safeguarding, securing, and maintaining facilities while cleanup is underway. The Office of Environmental Management also is responsible for the cleanup of DOE facilities that were involved in civilian nuclear energy research, which also generated wastes and contamination. These research facilities add a non-defense component to the office's mission, albeit smaller in terms of the scope of their cleanup and associated funding.[89]

Efforts to clean up the environmental legacy of nuclear weapons production and nuclear energy research represent the single largest environmental liability of the United States, exceeding the cleanup liability of Department of Defense facilities. The need for annual appropriations of several billion dollars for ongoing cleanup efforts at nuclear weapons production and nuclear energy research facilities has generated continuing interest within Congress about the long-term financial liability of the United States to address potential risks at these sites. How to ensure the protection of public safety, human health, and the environment in the most expedient and cost-effective manner has been a perennial issue in the appropriations debate.

DOE has identified in excess of 100 facilities in over 30 states that historically were involved in the production of nuclear weapons and nuclear energy research for civilian purposes.[90] The geographic scope of these facilities is substantial, collectively encompassing a land area of approximately 2 million acres. Cleanup remedies are in place and operational at the majority of these facilities. The responsibility for their long-term stewardship has been transferred to the Office of Legacy Management and other offices within DOE for the operation and maintenance of cleanup remedies and monitoring.[91] See the "Office of Legacy Management" section of this report. Some of the smaller sites for which DOE initially was responsible were transferred to the Army Corps of Engineers in 1997 under the Formerly Utilized Sites Remedial Action Program (FUSRAP). The cleanup of these sites is funded within the civil works budget of the Corps.[92]

---

[87] This section was prepared by David Bearden.

[88] In 1989, DOE created the Office of Environmental Restoration and Waste Management, which later was renamed the Office of Environmental Management.

[89] For additional information on the history, mission, and scope of the Office of Environmental Management, see DOE's website: http://energy.gov/em/office-environmental-management.

[90] For an interactive map and listing of each facility, see DOE's Office of Environmental Management website: http://energy.gov/em/cleanup-sites.

[91] The Office of Legacy Management administers the long-stewardship of DOE facilities that do not have a continuing mission once cleanup remedies are in place. Facilities that have a continuing mission are transferred to the DOE offices that administer those missions, which are responsible for their long-term stewardship.

[92] Enacted October 13, 1997, the Energy and Water Development Appropriations Act for FY1998 (P.L. 105-62) directed DOE to transfer the cleanup of 21 FUSRAP sites to the Army Corps of Engineers. DOE has remained (continued...)

(See **Table 4**.) Once the Corps completes the cleanup of a FUSRAP site, it is transferred back to DOE for long-term stewardship under the Office of Legacy Management.

Much work remains to be done at the facilities that are still administered by the Office of Environmental Management. DOE expects cleanup to continue for several years or even decades at some of these facilities, necessitating billions of dollars to fulfill the cleanup liability of the United States. As of the beginning of FY2013, the Office of Environmental Management had completed cleanup activities at 90 facilities in 30 states and the Commonwealth of Puerto Rico, and remains responsible for the cleanup of 17 facilities in 11 states at which cleanup was not yet complete.[93] Although cleanup is scheduled to be complete at some of these facilities over the next several years, cleanup is expected to continue at some of the larger and more complex facilities for decades. The Hanford facility in the state of Washington has the lengthiest estimated time frame, with cleanup scheduled to continue possibly as late as 2066 based on more conservative assumptions.[94] DOE estimates that the costs to complete the cleanup of these 17 facilities could range between $187.0 billion and $223.4 billion from FY2013 into the future, exceeding the past costs already incurred across the entire inventory of facilities.[95] A substantial proportion of these funding needs and lengthy time frames is due to challenges in managing, treating, and disposing of millions of gallons of high-level radioactive wastes stored in hundreds tanks at Hanford, the Savannah River facility in South Carolina, and the Idaho National Laboratory.

Over time, DOE periodically has revised its estimates as project baselines and assumptions change. These estimates have varied widely over the years by many billions of dollars. For example, the above estimates of future costs are several billion dollars higher than DOE presented just the previous fiscal year.[96] DOE typically estimates a range of costs, rather than a single dollar amount, to reflect uncertainties in the cleanup process. For example, final decisions have yet to be made at some facilities to determine the actions that will be necessary to remediate contamination. Methods to dispose of vast quantities of wastes, and the scheduling of these actions, also could affect cleanup costs and time frames. The costs of long-term stewardship also are excluded from the above cost estimates. Long-term stewardship entails an even greater degree of uncertainty considering the lengthy time frames of maintenance and monitoring once cleanup

---

(...continued)

responsible for determining the eligibility of additional sites, and Congress has designated certain sites in legislation.

[93] Department of Energy, Office of Chief Financial Officer, *FY2014 Congressional Budget Request*, April 2013, Volume 5, Environmental Management, p. EM-5 and EM-47. See page EM-47 for a list of the 17 facilities that still are administered by the Office of Environmental Management. One of these 17 facilities, the Waste Isolation Pilot Plant in New Mexico, is not a cleanup site, but is a permanent, geologic repository for "transuranic" wastes that are removed from other DOE facilities for disposal. The administration of the Hanford facility in the state of Washington is broken out into two DOE offices, the Office of River Protection and Richland Operations Office.

[94] Ibid. The projected completion dates for activities at the Hanford facility administered by the Richland Operations Office range from 2060 to 2066.

[95] Ibid., p. EM-23 and p. EM-46. DOE reports that the Office of Environmental Management has incurred $107.6 billion in past costs from FY1997 through FY2012. Including these past costs, the estimated total "life-cycle" costs of cleanup range from $294.6 billion to $330.9 billion. DOE has used FY1997 as the baseline, or starting point, for the time frame of these life-cycle estimates. Historically, DOE also has reported $35 billion in past costs incurred since the establishment of the Office of Environmental Management in 1989 through FY1996, yielding a total of $142.6 billion in past costs incurred from 1989 to FY2012. Comprehensive information on past costs incurred prior to the establishment of the Office of Environmental Management in 1989 is not readily available.

[96] Using FY2012 as a baseline or starting point, DOE had estimated remaining cleanup costs ranging from $174 billion to $209 billion in its FY2013 budget justification. See Department of Energy, Office of Chief Financial Officer, *FY2013 Congressional Budget Request*, February 2012, Volume 5, Environmental Management, p. 9.

---

remedies are in place and operational, especially at sites where the cleanup method may entail the permanent containment of radioactive wastes in perpetuity.

FY2014 appropriations proposed for the Office of Environmental Management and Office of Legacy Management are discussed separately below.

Table 15. Appropriations for the Office of Environmental Management

($ millions)

Account/Site or Program Activity	FY2012 Approp.	FY2013 Approp.	FY2014 Request	House	Senate	Conf.
Defense Environmental Cleanup						
Closure Sites	4.7	5.4	4.7	4.7	4.7	
Hanford	2,132.0	2,138.3	2,132.0	2,071.8	2,172.0	
- Richland Operations	950.0	953.3	921.8	876.6	961.8	
- Office of River Protection	1,182.0	1,185.0	1,210.2	1,195.2	1,210.2	
Idaho National Laboratory	384.7	386.9	365.0	368.0	380.0	
NNSA facilities and Nevada off-sites	282.0	282.4	309.7	284.9	344.7	
Oak Ridge Reservation	198.4	199.5	193.9a	204.0	214.9	
Savannah River Site	1,187.8	1,190.4	1,088.3	1,069.2	1,194.3	
Waste Isolation Pilot Plant	213.3	215.1	203.4	204.5	222.4	
Program Direction	321.6	321.6	280.8	280.8	320.8	
Program Support	20.4	20.4	18.0	18.0	18.0	
Safeguards and Security	251.0	252.0	234.1	234.1	250.7	
Technology Development and Deployment	10.3	11.0	24.0b	10.0	24.0	
Federal Payment to Uranium Enrichment D&D Fund	0.0	0.0	463.0	0.0	0.0	
H.Amdt. 249 to H.R. 2609	—	—	—	22.6	—	
Defense Environmental Cleanup Subtotal	**5,006.2**	**5,023.0**	**5,316.9**	**4,772.6c**	**5,146.5**	
Non-Defense Environmental Cleanup						
Fast Flux Test Reactor	2.7	2.7	2.5	2.5	2.5	
Gaseous Diffusion Plants	100.4	100.6	96.2	96.2	96.2	
Small Sites	67.5	67.4	50.2	48.2	70.2	
West Valley Demonstration Project	64.7	65.0	64.0	47.0	64.0	
H.Amdt. 268 to H.R. 2609	—	—	—	19.0	—	
Non-Defense Environmental Cleanup Subtotal	**235.4**	**235.7**	**213.0**	**213.0d**	**233.0**	
Uranium Enrichment D&D Fund						
Gaseous Diffusion Plants	472.2	472.9	530.9	545.0	530.9	
- Oak Ridge	200.9	200.9	177.1	186.2	177.1	
- Paducah	81.4	81.8	262.1	265.2	262.1	
- Portsmouth	190.0	190.3	91.8	93.6	91.8	
Pension, Community, and Regulatory Supporte	—	—	23.9	—	23.9	
Uranium Enrichment D&D Fund Subtotal	**472.2**	**472.9**	**554.8**	**545.0**	**554.8**	

Account/Site or Program Activity	FY2012 Approp.	FY2013 Approp.	FY2014 Request	House	Senate	Conf.
Use of Prior Year Defense Environmental Cleanup Funds	-3.4	0.0	0.0	0.0	0.0	
Offset for Federal Payment to Uranium Enrichment D&D Fund	0.0	0.0	-463.0	0.0	0.0	
Office of Environmental Management Total	**5,710.4**	**5,731.6**	**5,621.7**	**5,530.6**	**5,934.3**	

Source: Prepared by the Congressional Research Service using information from the House Appropriations Committee report on H.R. 2609 (H.Rept. 113-135) including pre-sequester FY2013 enacted appropriations, House floor amendments to H.R. 2609, the Senate Appropriations Committee report on S. 1245 (S.Rept. 113-47), and the Department of Energy, Office of Chief Financial Officer, *FY2014 Congressional Budget Request*, April 2013, Volume 5, Environmental Management. Numbers may not add due to rounding.

a. H.Rept. 113-135 presented a different accounting of the President's FY2014 request for the Oak Ridge Reservation, citing $198.0 million. S.Rept. 113-47 cited $193.9 million as in DOE's budget justification.

b. H.Rept. 113-135 presented a different accounting of the President's FY2014 request for Technology Development, citing $20.0 million. S.Rept. 113-47 cited $24.1 million as in DOE's budget justification.

c. As passed by the House, H.Amdt. 249 to H.R. 2609 increased the total amount for the Defense Environmental Cleanup account by an additional $22,586,500.

d. As passed by the House, H.Amdt. 268 to H.R. 2609 increased the total amount for the Non-Defense Environmental Cleanup account by an additional $18,956,000.

e. Pension, Community, and Regulatory Support is broken out in the Uranium Enrichment D&D Fund in DOE's budget justification and in S.Rept. 113-47. This activity received funding within the account total in FY2012 and FY2013, and for FY2014 in H.Rept. 113-135, but was not broken out in those instances.

Office of Environmental Management

Three appropriations accounts fund the Office of Environmental Management: Defense Environmental Cleanup, Non-Defense Environmental Cleanup, and the Uranium Enrichment Decontamination and Decommissioning (D&D) Fund. The Defense Environmental Cleanup account constitutes the vast majority of the funding for the Office of Environmental Management and is devoted to the cleanup of former nuclear weapons production facilities. The Non-Defense Environmental Cleanup account funds the cleanup of wastes and contamination resulting from civilian nuclear energy research. Title XI of the Energy Policy Act of 1992 (P.L. 102-486) established the Uranium Enrichment D&D Fund to pay for the cleanup of three federal facilities that were used to enrich uranium for national defense and civilian purposes and to reimburse uranium and thorium licensees for their costs of cleaning up sites that supported these facilities.[97] These three federal uranium enrichment facilities are located in Paducah, Kentucky; Piketon, Ohio (Portsmouth plant); and Oak Ridge, Tennessee.

As passed by the House, H.R. 2609 would provide a total of $5.53 billion for these three accounts combined to fund the Office of Environmental Management in FY2014, $403.7 million less than the total of $5.93 billion included in S. 1245 as reported by the Senate Appropriations Committee. The President had requested $5.62 billion for the Office of Environmental Management in FY2014, $91.1 million more than the House proposed and $312.6 million less than the Senate Appropriations Committee recommended. In comparison to the prior fiscal year, Congress appropriated $5.73 billion for the Office of Environmental Management in FY2013 (pre-sequester as reported by the House Appropriations Committee).

---

[97] 42 U.S.C. §2297g.

The House floor debate over FY2014 appropriations for the Office of Environmental Management focused on the prioritization of funding for the cleanup of nuclear weapons production and nuclear energy research facilities among other competing priorities within DOE's mission, including research, renewable energy, energy efficiency, and administration of DOE programs and activities. The House-passed funding level of $5.53 billion for the Office of Environmental Management includes $41.5 million more than the House Appropriations Committee had recommended in its report on H.R. 2609. This funding was added through two amendments approved in floor debate, accompanied by offsets to other DOE accounts to remain within the budget allocation for the bill.

H.Amdt. 249 increased the Defense Environmental Cleanup account by $22.6 million with offsetting reductions in the Departmental Administration account and the Renewable Energy, Energy Reliability and Efficiency account. Floor statements indicated that the $22.6 million increase is intended to restore a portion of the reduction for the Richland Operations Office at the Hanford facility.[98] As reported by the House Appropriations Committee, the bill would have decreased funding for this DOE office by $45.1 million below the President's request and by $76.6 million below the FY2013 enacted level (pre-sequester).[99]

H.Amdt. 268 increased the Non-Defense Environmental Cleanup account by $19.0 million with offsetting reductions in the Departmental Administration account and the Office of the Administrator account for the National Nuclear Security Administration within DOE. Floor statements indicated that the $19.0 million increase for the Non-Defense Environmental Cleanup account is intended to restore a portion of the $41.7 million reduction below the FY2013 enacted level (pre-sequester) that the House Appropriations Committee had recommended.[100] The $19.0 million added by the amendment would increase the Non-Defense Environmental Cleanup account to the full level that the President had requested, of which $17.0 million would be devoted to the West Valley Demonstration Project site in the state of New York.[101]

Although there are varied issues among individual DOE facilities, the overall adequacy of funding for the Office of Environmental Management to attain cleanup milestones across the facility inventory has been an overarching issue. Cleanup milestones are enforceable measures incorporated into compliance agreements negotiated among DOE, the Environmental Protection Agency (EPA), and the states. These milestones establish time frames for the completion of specific actions to satisfy applicable requirements at individual facilities.[102] According to DOE, the President's request for the Office of Environmental Management would be sufficient to attain all cleanup milestones due in FY2014.[103] In its report on H.R. 2609, the House Appropriations Committee noted the "need to ensure progress toward cleanup milestones" and stated that the bill would "sustain the pace of cleanup across the sites."[104] The Senate Appropriations Committee asserted that the House markup "would cause major cleanup milestones to be missed in

---

[98] See *Congressional Record*, House, July 9, 2013, p. H4256.

[99] See H.Rept. 113-135, p. 170.

[100] See *Congressional Record*, House, July 9, 2013, p. H4279.

[101] See H.Rept. 113-135, p. 155.

[102] Compliance agreements for individual facilities are available on DOE's Office of Environmental Management website: http://energy.gov/em/compliance-agreements.

[103] Department of Energy, Office of Chief Financial Officer, *FY2014 Congressional Budget Request*, April 2013, Volume 5, Environmental Management, p. EM-6.

[104] See H.Rept. 113-135, p. 138.

Washington, New Mexico, South Carolina, Idaho, and Tennessee."[105] As noted above, two floor amendments to H.R. 2609 subsequently provided an additional $41.5 million to make up some of the proposed reductions below the President's request.

Neither H.R. 2609 as passed by the House, nor S. 1245 as reported by the Senate Appropriations Committee, includes the $463 million that the President requested within the Defense Environmental Cleanup account to resume the federal payment to the Uranium Enrichment D&D Fund. Congress ceased the federal payment in FY2012. This payment historically has been treated as an offset to the funding for the Office of Environmental Management because the payment does not become available to DOE until Congress subsequently appropriates it out of the Uranium Enrichment D&D Fund. The President also has proposed to resume assessments on nuclear utilities in FY2014 to generate additional revenues.[106] The authority to collect these assessments expired in October 2007. As authorized in the Energy Policy Act of 1992, both federal payments and nuclear utility assessments originally financed the Uranium Enrichment D&D Fund based on the premise that the federal government and the nuclear utilities benefited from services provided by federal uranium enrichment facilities and that both therefore should share the costs of the cleanup of these facilities.

The Office of Management and Budget (OMB) estimated an existing balance of $3.5 billion in the Uranium Enrichment D&D Fund accrued from past nuclear utility assessments and federal payments that would be available for appropriation in FY2014.[107] Appropriations proposed in H.R. 2609 and S. 1245 still would leave roughly $3.0 billion for appropriation in future fiscal years (plus accrued interest on the balance). DOE last estimated in 2010 that the balance of the fund would be exhausted by FY2020 without additional revenues, leaving a shortfall of $11.8 billion to complete the cleanup of federal uranium enrichment facilities over the long term.[108] If the Uranium Enrichment D&D Fund were fully expended, existing law requires DOE still to pay the costs of cleanup, subject to annual appropriations.[109]

Among the individual DOE facilities and supporting program activities, appropriations proposals for the Office of Environmental Management in FY2014 reflect differing priorities. **Table □□** presents the three appropriations accounts that fund the Office of Environmental Management with a breakout by facility and program activity. The table presents the amounts proposed for FY2014 in H.R. 2609 as passed by the House, S. 1245 as reported by the Senate Appropriations Committee, and the President's budget request, compared to appropriations enacted for FY2012 and FY2013 (pre-sequester as reported by the House Appropriations Committee). The table also presents the net total program funding level for the Office of Environmental Management for the three accounts combined, accounting for offsets including the federal payment to the Uranium Enrichment D&D Fund that the President proposed to resume in FY2014.

---

[105] See the Senate Appropriations Committee June 27, 2013 press release on the full committee markup of S. 1245, http://www.appropriations.senate.gov/news.cfm?method=news.view&id=ba47a4ea-f6df-4341-9716-89343ce3e8c6.

[106] Office of Management and Budget, *FY2014 Budget of the U.S. Government*, Analytical Perspectives, p. 209.

[107] Office of Management and Budget, *FY2014 Budget of the U.S. Government*, Appendix, p. 397.

[108] Department of Energy, *Uranium Enrichment Decontamination and Decommissioning Report for Congress*, December 2010, p. 42. The Energy Policy Act of 1992 requires DOE to report to Congress on the financial status of the Uranium Enrichment D&D Fund every three years.

[109] 42 U.S.C. §2297g-2(c).

Office of Legacy Management

Once cleanup remedies are in place under the Office of Environmental Management, DOE's Office of Legacy Management administers the long-term stewardship of the facilities that do not have a continuing mission. The Office of Legacy Management also is responsible for the long-term stewardship of sites that had been transferred from DOE to the Army Corps of Engineers under the FUSRAP program in 1997. Once the Corps completes the cleanup of a site under this program, it is responsible for the initial two years of operation and maintenance, after which time the site is transferred back to DOE's Office of Legacy Management for long-term stewardship.[110]

The Office of Legacy Management also manages the payment of pensions and retirement benefits of former contractor personnel who worked at DOE facilities that do not have a continuing mission,[111] among other supporting activities.[112] The federal role in the management of these former contractor pensions and benefits stems from the long-term nature of the projects and the associated length of employment for the personnel who performed the work for DOE. These pensions and benefits are earned and accrued by contractor employees while in active employment at DOE facilities and are payable after their employment ends.[113]

The Office of Legacy Management has been funded entirely within DOE's Other Defense Activities account since FY2009.[114] As passed by the House, H.R. 2609 would provide $173.0 million within this account for the Office of Legacy Management in FY2014. As reported by the Senate Appropriations Committee, S. 1245 would provide $177.0 million, the same amount as the President requested. These proposed amounts would be an increase above the enacted appropriations of $169.6 million in FY2013 (pre-sequester).

During FY2014, the Office of Legacy Management plans to continue its management of three major closure sites and almost 90 other small sites, and to add six new sites to its inventory for long-term stewardship responsibility by the end of that fiscal year.[115] DOE reports that funding needs for new sites, other new actions, and inflationary increases for various program elements have been partially offset in the near term through improvements in program and administrative efficiencies and a decrease in the need to contribute to former contractor workers' pension funds.[116] However, funding needs for the Office of Legacy Management are likely to increase

---

[110] Memorandum of Understanding Between the U.S. Department Of Energy and the U.S. Army Corps Of Engineers Regarding Program Administration and Execution of the Formerly Utilized Sites Remedial Action Program (FUSRAP), March 1999.

[111] Similar to long-term stewardship responsibilities, the payment of pensions and post-retirement benefits of workers at facilities with a continuing DOE mission is assigned to the program office within DOE that is responsible for administering that mission, rather than the Office of Legacy Management.

[112] For more information on the history, mission, and scope of the Office of Legacy Management, see DOE's website: http://energy.gov/lm/office-legacy-management.

[113] For more information on DOE's management of former contractor pensions and benefits, see the Office of Legacy Management Post-Closure Benefits Program website: http://www.lm.doe.gov/default.aspx?id=172.

[114] Prior to FY2009, Congress appropriated funding for the relatively small number of non-defense facilities administered by the Office of Legacy Management within a stand-alone account. The majority of the facilities administered by this office were involved in the U.S. nuclear weapons program, but some of the facilities were contaminated by civilian nuclear energy research activities.

[115] Department of Energy, Office of Chief Financial Officer, *FY2014 Congressional Budget Request,* April 2013, Volume 2, Other Defense Activities, p. ODA-39.

[116] Ibid., p. ODA-40.

---

more significantly over the next decade, as additional facilities are cleaned up and transferred from the Office of Environmental Management and the FUSRAP program for long-term stewardship. Over the next 10 years, DOE projects that the total number of facilities administered by the Office of Legacy Management will rise from 91 in FY2011 to 129 in FY2020.[117]

Estimating the long-term funding needs for the Office of Legacy Management is inherently challenging because of the lengthy time horizons that are involved. For example, actions may be necessary for many decades to operate and maintain cleanup remedies and monitor contaminant levels to ensure the effectiveness of the remedies over time. At sites where the cleanup entails the permanent containment of radioactive wastes, long-term stewardship may continue indefinitely because of the time needed for radioactivity to decay to acceptable levels. Enforcement of land use restrictions or other institutional controls also may be necessary in perpetuity at facilities that are not cleaned up for unrestricted use, in order to prevent potentially harmful exposures. These and other factors make it difficult to reliably estimate the financial liability of the United States for long-term stewardship of sites contaminated from the historic production of nuclear weapons and civilian nuclear energy research in the 20th century.[118]

Power Marketing Administrations[119]

DOE's four Power Marketing Administrations (PMAs)—Bonneville Power Administration (BPA), Southeastern Power Administration (SEPA), Southwestern Power Administration (SWPA), and Western Area Power Administration (WAPA)—were established to sell the power generated by the dams operated by the Bureau of Reclamation and the Army Corps of Engineers. In many cases, conservation and management of water resources—including irrigation, flood control, recreation, or other objectives—were the primary purpose of federal projects. (For more information, see CRS Report RS22564, *Power Marketing Administrations: Background and Current Issues*, by Richard J. Campbell.)

Priority for PMA power is extended to "preference customers," which include municipal utilities, cooperatives, and other "public" bodies. The PMAs sell power to these entities "at the lowest possible rates" consistent with what they describe as "sound business practice." The PMAs are responsible for covering their expenses and for repaying debt and the federal investment in the generating facilities.

The Obama Administration's FY2014 request for the PMAs was $85 million. This is the same level as the FY2012 appropriation. The FY2014 budget request continues a change enacted in FY2010 that reclassified receipts from the PMAs from mandatory to discretionary. This change offsets many of the expenses of WAPA, SWPA, and SEPA that were previously paid for with discretionary appropriations. As a result of the change, two PMAs require discretionary funding in addition to their receipts: SWPA requests $11.9 million and WAPA requests $95.9 million.

---

[117] Department of Energy, Office of Legacy Management, *2011-2020 Strategic Plan*, DOE/LM-0512, January 2011, p. 5, available on DOE's website: http://energy.gov/lm/downloads/2011-2020-strategic-plan.

[118] DOE annually estimates the financial liabilities of long-term stewardship as a portion of other environmental liabilities of the department, but does not report a separate estimate just for long-term stewardship alone. Furthermore, DOE estimates these liabilities only for the first 75 years and acknowledges that costs are likely to be incurred beyond this time frame that "cannot reasonably be estimated." See Department of Energy, *Fiscal Year 2012 Agency Financial Report*, November 2012, "Environmental Cleanup and Disposal Liabilities," p. 62-64, available on DOE's website: http://energy.gov/sites/prod/files/2012parafr_0.pdf.

[119] This section was prepared by Charles V. Stern.

Receipts for SEPA are expected to offset all operating costs in FY2011. In addition, $400,000 is requested for Falcon and Amistad operations and maintenance, and collections of $23 million from Colorado River basins score as an additional offset toward the net discretionary appropriation. Both the House and the Senate bills would appropriate the requested amount for PMAs.

BPA is a self-funded agency under authority granted by P.L. 93-454 (16 U.S.C. §838), the Federal Columbia River Transmission System Act of 1974, and receives no appropriations. However, it funds some of its activities from permanent borrowing authority with the Treasury, which was increased in FY2003 from $3.75 billion to $4.45 billion (a $700 million increase). ARRA further increased the amount of borrowing that BPA conducts under the Transmission System Act by $3.25 billion to the current authority for $7.7 billion in bonds outstanding to the Treasury.

ARRA also provided WAPA borrowing authority for the purpose of planning, financing or building new or upgraded electric power transmission lines to facilitate the delivery of renewable energy resources constructed by or expected to be constructed after the date of enactment. The authority to borrow from the United States Treasury had not previously been available to WAPA. It is now available on a permanent, indefinite basis, with the amount of borrowing outstanding not to exceed $3.25 billion.

Title IV: Independent Agencies

Independent agencies that receive funding from the Energy and Water Development bill include the Nuclear Regulatory Commission (NRC), the Appalachian Regional Commission (ARC), and the Denali Commission.

Table 16. Energy and Water Development Appropriations
Title IV: Independent Agencies
($ millions)

Program	FY2013[a] Approp.	FY2014 Request	House	Senate	Conf.
Appalachian Regional Commission	$68.1	$64.6	70.3	68.2	
Nuclear Regulatory Commission	1,036.0	1,055.0	1,055.0	1,055.0	
(Revenues)	-909.5	-930.7	-930.7	-930.7	
Net NRC (including Inspector General)	126.5	124.3	124.3	124.3	
Defense Nuclear Facilities Safety Board	29.1	29.9	29.9	29.9	
Nuclear Waste Technical Review Board	3.4	3.0	3.0	3.0	
Denali Commission	10.7	7.0	7.0	10.0	
Delta Regional Authority	11.7	11.0	11.0	12.0	
Northern Border Regional Commission	1.5	1.0	1.0	5.0	
Southern Crescent Regional Commission	0.3	0.0	0.3	0.0	
Fed. Coord. Alaska Gas Projects	1.0	3.0	3.0	1.0	
Total	**252.2**	**243.8**	**249.3**	**253.8**	

Source: FY2014 budget request, H.Rept. 113-135, S.Rept. 113-47.

Notes: Figures may not add due to rounding.

a. Source: H.Rept. 113-135. Figures do not reflect the March 1, 2013, sequester of funds under P.L. 112-25.

Key Policy Issues—Independent Agencies

Nuclear Regulatory Commission[120]

The Nuclear Regulatory Commission (NRC) requested $1.055 billion for FY2014 (including $11.1 million for the inspector general's office), $16.9 million above the FY2012 funding level. Major activities conducted by NRC include safety regulation and licensing of commercial nuclear reactors and oversight of nuclear materials users.[121] The House bill included the same amount, as did the Senate Appropriations Committee recommendation.

The NRC budget request includes $240.5 million for new reactor activities, $24.9 million below the FY2012 level. Until 2007, no new commercial reactor construction applications had been submitted to NRC since the 1970s. However, volatile fossil fuel prices, the possibility of controls on carbon emissions, and incentives provided by the Energy Policy Act of 2005 prompted electric utilities and other generating companies to apply for licenses for 30 new reactors. Several of those applications were subsequently withdrawn or suspended, though, as falling natural gas prices reduced the competitiveness of nuclear power. NRC issued combined construction and operating licenses for four new reactors at two sites in Georgia and South Carolina in early 2012.

NRC's proposed FY2014 budget includes no funds for licensing DOE's previously planned Yucca Mountain nuclear waste repository. Because the Obama Administration wants to cancel the Yucca Mountain project and filed a motion to withdraw the license application on March 3, 2010, the NRC's FY2011 appropriation was used to close out its licensing activities. As discussed in the Nuclear Waste section of this report, the U.S. Court of Appeals for the District of Columbia Circuit ordered NRC on August 13, 2013, to continue reviewing the Yucca Mountain license application, using $11.1 million in leftover funding. Similarly, the House Appropriations Committee directed NRC to use prior-year funds to complete the Yucca Mountain license application, and contended that NRC was required by law to find additional resources as needed.

For regulation of operating reactors, NRC's FY2014 budget request includes $571.9 million, $37.2 million above the FY2012 level. Those activities include reactor safety inspections, license renewals and modifications, collection and analysis of reactor performance data, and oversight of security exercises. The Fukushima nuclear disaster in Japan increased congressional and public concern about the safety of U.S. nuclear power plants. NRC established a task force 10 days after the accident to review NRC's regulatory system. NRC issued the first regulatory orders resulting from that review on March 12, 2012, and is currently working on additional regulations.[122]

---

[120] This section was prepared by Mark Holt.

[121] U.S. Nuclear Regulatory Commission, *FY 2013 Congressional Budget Justification*, NUREG-1100, Vol. 28, February 2012, http://www.nrc.gov/reading-rm/doc-collections/nuregs/staff/sr1100/v28/fy2013-cbj.pdf.

[122] U.S. Nuclear Regulatory Commission, "Actions in Response to the Japan Nuclear Accident," http://www.nrc.gov/japan/japan-info.html. For a timeline of NRC actions, see http://www.nrc.gov/reactors/operating/ops-experience/japan/japan-timeline.html.

The Energy Policy Act of 2005 permanently extended a requirement that 90% of NRC's budget be offset by fees on licensees. Not subject to the offset are expenditures from the Nuclear Waste Fund to pay for waste repository licensing, spending on general homeland security, and DOE defense waste oversight. The offsets in the FY2014 request would result in a net appropriation of $124.3 million, $4.3 million below the FY2012 enacted level.

Author Contact Information

Carl E. Behrens, Coordinator
Specialist in Energy Policy
cbehrens@crs.loc.gov, 7-8303

Anthony Andrews
Specialist in Energy Policy
aandrews@crs.loc.gov, 7-6843

David M. Bearden
Specialist in Environmental Policy
dbearden@crs.loc.gov, 7-2390

Carol Glover
Information Research Specialist
cglover@crs.loc.gov, 7-7353

Heather B. Gonzalez
Specialist in Science and Technology Policy
hgonzalez@crs.loc.gov, 7-1895

Mark Holt
Specialist in Energy Policy
mholt@crs.loc.gov, 7-1704

Jonathan E. Medalia
Specialist in Nuclear Weapons Policy
jmedalia@crs.loc.gov, 7-7632

Fred Sissine
Specialist in Energy Policy
fsissine@crs.loc.gov, 7-7039

Charles V. Stern
Specialist in Natural Resources Policy
cstern@crs.loc.gov, 7-7786

Key Policy Staff

Area of Expertise	Name	Phone	E-mail
General	Carl Behrens	7-8303	cbehrens@crs.loc.gov
	Carol Glover	7-7353	cglover@crs.loc.gov
Corps of Engineers	Charles V. Stern	7-7786	cstern@crs.loc.gov
	Nicole Carter	7-0854	ncarter@crs.loc.gov
Bureau of Reclamation	Charles V. Stern	7-7786	cstern@crs.loc.gov
	Betsy Cody	7-7229	bcody@crs.loc.gov
Solar and Renewable Energy	Fred Sissine	7-7039	fsissine@crs.loc.gov
Nuclear Energy	Mark Holt	7-1704	mholt@crs.loc.gov
Science Programs	Heather B. Gonzalez	7-1895	hgonzalez@crs.loc.gov
Nuclear Weapons Stewardship	Jonathan Medalia	7-7632	jmedalia@crs.loc.gov
Nonproliferation	Carl Behrens	7-8303	cbehrens@crs.loc.gov
DOE Environmental Management	David Bearden	7-2390	dbearden@crs.loc.gov
Power Marketing Administrations	Charles V. Stern	7-7786	cstern@crs.loc.gov

Area of Expertise	Name	Phone	E-mail
Bonneville Power Administration	Charles V. Stern	7-7786	cstern@crs.loc.gov
Fossil Energy Research	Anthony Andrews	7-6843	aandrews@crs.loc.gov
Strategic Petroleum Reserve	Anthony Andrews	7-6843	aandrews@crs.loc.gov
Energy Conservation	Fred Sissine	7-7039	fsissine@crs.loc.gov
Budget Data	Carol Glover	7-7353	cglover@crs.loc.gov